HOTEL
SPLENDIDE

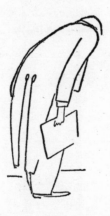

Also by this author

---•---

To the One I Love the Best

HOTEL SPLENDIDE

Pushkin Press

LUDWIG BEMELMANS

Pushkin Press
65–69 Shelton Street
London wc2h 9he

Hotel Splendide was first published in 1941

First published by Pushkin Press in 2022

1 3 5 7 9 8 6 4 2

ISBN 13: 978-1-78227-791-0

Designed and typeset by Tetragon, London
Printed and bound by Clays Ltd, Elcograf S.p.A.

www.pushkinpress.com

HOTEL
SPLENDIDE

Contents

———— • ————

I

The Animal Waiter

The day was one of the rare ones when Mespoulets and I had a guest at our tables. Most of the time I mugged into a large mirror in back of me. Mespoulets stood next to me and shook his head. Mespoulets was a waiter and I was his bus boy. Our station was on the low rear balcony of the main dining-room of a hotel I shall call the Splendide, a vast and luxurious structure with many mirrors which gave up its unequal struggle with economics not long after the boom days and has since most probably been converted into an office building or torn down.

Before coming to America I had worked a short while in a hotel in Tirol that belonged to my uncle. German was my native language, and I knew enough English to get along in New York City, but my French was extremely bad. The French language in all its aspects was a passion with Mespoulets, and he had plenty of time to teach it to me.

'When I say "*Le chien est utile*," there is one proposition. When I say "*Je crois que le chien est utile*," there are two. When I say "*Je crois que le chien est utile quand il garde la maison*," how many propositions are there?'

'Three.'

'Very good.'

Mespoulets nodded gravely in approval. At that moment Monsieur Victor, the *maître d'hôtel*, walked through our section of tables, and the other waiters nearby stopped talking to each other, straightened a table-cloth here, moved a chair there, arranged their side towels smoothly over their arms, tugged at their jackets, and pulled their bow ties. Only Mespoulets was indifferent. He walked slowly towards the pantry, past Monsieur Victor, holding my arm. I walked with him and he continued the instruction.

'"*L'abeille fait du miel*." The verb "*fait*" in this sentence in itself is insufficient. It does not say what the bee does, therefore we round out the idea by adding the words "*du miel*". These words are called "*un complément*". The sentence "*L'abeille fait du miel*" contains then what?'

'It contains one verb, one subject, and one complement.'

'Very good, excellent. Now run down and get the Camembert, the *salade escarole*, the hard water crackers, and the demitasse for Mr Frank Munsey on Table Eighty-six.'

Our tables – Nos. 81, 82, and 86 – were in a noisy, draughty corner of the balcony. They stood facing the stairs from the dining-room and were between two doors. One door led to the pantry and was hung on whining hinges. On wet days it sounded like an angry cat and it was continually kicked by the boots of waiters rushing in and out with trays in their hands. The other door led to a linen-closet.

The waiters and bus boys squeezed by our tables, carrying trays. The ones with trays full of food carried them high over their heads; the ones with dirty dishes carried them low, extended in front. They frequently bumped into each other and there would be a crash of silver, glasses, and china, and cream trickling over the edges of the trays in thin streams. Whenever this happened, Monsieur Victor raced to our section, followed by his captains, to direct the cleaning up of the mess and pacify the guests. It was a common sight to see people standing in our section, napkins in hand, complaining and brushing themselves off and waving their arms angrily in the air.

Monsieur Victor used our tables as a kind of penal colony to which he sent guests who were notorious cranks, people who had forgotten to tip him over a long period of time and needed a reminder, undesirables who looked out of place in better sections of the dining-room, and guests who were known to linger for hours over an order of hors d'œuvres and a glass of milk while well-paying guests had to stand at the door waiting for a table.

Mespoulets was the ideal man for Monsieur Victor's purposes. He complemented Monsieur Victor's plan of punishment. He was probably the worst waiter in the world, and I had become his bus boy after I fell down the stairs into the main part of the dining-room with eight pheasants *à la Souvaroff*. When I was sent to him to take up my duties as his assistant, he introduced himself by saying, 'My name is easy to remember. Just think of "my chickens" – "*mes poulets*" – Mespoulets.'

Rarely did any guest who was seated at one of our tables leave the hotel with a desire to come back again. If there was any broken glass around the dining-room, it was always in our spinach. The occupants of Tables Nos. 81, 82, and 86 shifted in their chairs, stared at the pantry door, looked around and made signs of distress at other waiters and captains while they waited for their food. When the food finally came, it was cold and was often not what had been ordered. While Mespoulets explained what the unordered food was, telling in detail how it was made and what the ingredients were, and offered hollow excuses, he dribbled mayonnaise, soup, or mint sauce over the guests, upset the coffee, and sometimes even managed to break a plate or two. I helped him as best I could.

At the end of a meal, Mespoulets usually presented the guest with somebody else's check, or it turned out that he had neglected to adjust the difference in price between what the guest had ordered and what he had got. By then the guest just held out his hand and cried, 'Never mind, never mind, give it to me, just give it to me! I'll pay just to get out of here! Give it to me, for God's sake!' Then the guest would pay and go. He would stop on the way out at the *maître d'hôtel*'s desk and show Monsieur Victor and his captains the spots on his clothes, bang on the desk, and swear he would never come back again. Monsieur Victor and his captains would listen, make faces of compassion, say 'Oh!' and 'Ah!' and look darkly towards us across the room and promise that we would be fired the same day. But the next day we would still be there.

In the hours between meals, while the other waiters were occupied filling salt and pepper shakers, oil and vinegar bottles, and mustard pots, and counting the dirty linen and dusting the chairs, Mespoulets would walk to a table near the entrance, right next to Monsieur Victor's own desk, overlooking the lounge of the hotel. There he adjusted a special reading-lamp which he had demanded and obtained from the management, spread a piece of billiard cloth over the table, and arranged on top of this a large blotter and a small one, an inkstand, and half a dozen pen-holders. Then he drew up a chair and seated himself. He had a large assortment of fine copper pen-points of various sizes, and he sharpened them on a piece of sand-paper. He would select the pen-point and the holder he wanted and begin to make circles in the air. Then, drawing towards him a gilt-edged place card or a crested one, on which menus were written, he would go to work. When he had finished, he arranged the cards all over the table to let them dry, and sat there at ease, only a step or two from Monsieur Victor's desk, in a sector invaded by other waiters only when they were to be called down or to be discharged, waiters who came with nervous hands and frightened eyes to face Monsieur Victor. Mespoulets's special talent guaranteed him his job and set him apart from the ordinary waiters. He was further distinguished by the fact that he was permitted to wear glasses, a privilege denied all other waiters, no matter how near-sighted or astigmatic.

It was said of Mespoulets variously that he was the father, the uncle, or the brother of Monsieur Victor. It was also said of him that he had once been the director of a lycée in Paris. The truth was that he had never known Monsieur Victor on the other side, and I do not think there was any secret between them, only an understanding, a subtle sympathy of some kind. I learned that he had once been a tutor to a family in which there was a very beautiful daughter and that this was something he did not like to talk about. He loved animals almost as dearly as he loved the French language. He had taken it upon himself to watch over the fish which were in an aquarium in the outer lobby of the hotel, he fed the pigeons in the courtyard, and he extended his interest to the birds and beasts and crustaceans that came alive to the kitchen. He begged the cooks to deal quickly, as painlessly as could be, with lobsters and terrapins. If a guest brought a dog to our section, Mespoulets was mostly under the table with the dog.

At mealtime, while we waited for the few guests who came our way, Mespoulets sat out in the linen-closet on a small box where he could keep an eye on our tables through the partly open door. He leaned comfortably against a pile of table-cloths and napkins. At his side was an ancient *Grammaire Française*, and while his hands were folded in his lap, the palms up, the thumbs cruising over them in small, silent circles, he made me repeat exercises, simple, compact, and easy to remember. He knew them all by heart, and soon I did, too. He made me go over and over them until my pronunciation was right. All of them were about animals. There were: 'The Sage Salmon', 'The Cat and the Old Woman', 'The Society of Beavers', 'The Bear in the Swiss Mountains', 'The Intelligence of the Partridge', 'The Lion of Florence', and 'The Bird in the Cage'.

We started with 'The Sage Salmon' in January that year and were at the end of 'The Bear in the Swiss Mountains' when the summer garden opened in May. At that season business fell off for dinner, and all during the summer we were busy only at luncheon. Mespoulets had time to go home in the afternoons and he suggested that I continue studying there.

He lived in the house of a relative on West Twenty-fourth Street. On the sidewalk in front of the house next door stood a large wooden horse, painted red, the sign of a saddle-maker. Across the street was a place where horses were auctioned off, and up the block was an Italian poultry market with a picture of a chicken painted on its front. Hens and roosters crowded the market every morning.

Mespoulets occupied a room and bath on the second floor rear. The room was papered green and over an old couch hung a print of Van Gogh's *Bridge at Arles*, which was not a common picture then. There were bookshelves, a desk covered with papers, and over the desk a large bird-cage hanging from the ceiling.

In this cage, shaded with a piece of the hotel's billiard cloth, lived a miserable old canary. It was bald-headed, its eyes were like peppercorns, its feet were no longer able to cling to the roost, and it sat in the sand, in a corner, looking like a withered chrysanthemum that had been thrown away. On summer afternoons, near the bird, we studied 'The Intelligence of the Partridge' and 'The Lion of Florence'.

Late in August, on a chilly day that seemed like fall, Mespoulets and I began 'The Bird in the Cage'. The lesson was:

L'OISEAU EN CAGE

Voilà sur ma fenêtre un oiseau qui vient visiter le mien. Il a peur, il s'en va, et le pauvre prisonnier s'attriste, s'agite comme pour s'échapper. Je ferais comme lui, si j'étais à sa place, et cependant je le retiens. Vais-je lui ouvrir? Il irait voler, chanter, faire son nid; il serait heureux; mais je ne l'aurais plus, et je l'aime, et je veux l'avoir. Je le garde. Pauvre petit, tu seras toujours

prisonnier; je jouis de toi aux dépens de ta liberté, je te plains,
et je te garde. Voilà comme le plaisir l'emporte sur la justice.

I translated for him: 'There's a bird at my window, come to visit
mine. … The poor prisoner is sad. … I would feel as he does,
if I were in his place, yet I keep him. … Poor prisoner, I enjoy
you at the cost of your liberty … pleasure before justice."

Mespoulets looked up at the bird and said to me, 'Find some
adjective to use with *"fenêtre"*, *"oiseau"*, *"liberté"*, *"plaisir"*,
and *"justice"*,' and while I searched for them in our diction-
ary, he went to a shelf and took from it a cigar-box. There
was one cigar in it. He took this out, wiped off the box with
his handkerchief, and then went to a drawer and got a large
penknife, which he opened. He felt the blade. Then he went
to the cage, took the bird out, laid it on the closed cigar-box,
and quickly cut off its head. One claw opened slowly and the
bird and its head lay still.

Mespoulets washed his hands, rolled the box, the bird, and
the knife into a newspaper, put it under his arm, and took
his hat from a stand. We went out and walked up Eighth
Avenue. At Thirty-fourth Street he stopped at a trash-can
and put his bundle into it. 'I don't think he wanted to live
any more,' he said.

II

Art at the Hotel Splendide

'From now on,' lisped Monsieur Victor, as if he were pinning on me the Grand Cross of the Legion of Honour, 'you will be a waiter.'

It was about a year after I had gone to work at the Splendide as Mespoulets's bus boy, and only a month or two after I had been promoted to *commis*. A *commis* feels more self-satisfied than a bus boy and has a better life all around, but to become a waiter is to make a really worthwhile progress.

The cause of my promotion was a waiters' mutiny. On a rainy afternoon several of the waiters had suddenly thrown down their napkins and aprons and walked out. One had punched the chief bus boy in the nose and another had upset a tray filled with Spode demitasse cups. They wanted ten dollars a week instead of six; they wanted to do away with certain penalties that were imposed on them, such as a fine of fifty cents for using a serving napkin to clean an ashtray; and they wanted a full day off instead of having to come back on their free day to serve dinner, which was the custom at the Splendide, as at most other New York hotels. The good waiters did not go on strike. A few idealists spoke too loudly and got fired, and a lot of bad waiters, who had mediocre stations, left.

After my promotion I was stationed at the far end of the room, on the 'undesirables" balcony, and my two tables were next to Mespoulets's.

It rained all that first day and all the next, and there were no guests on the bad balcony. With nothing to do, Mespoulets and I stood and looked at the ceiling, talked, or sat on overturned linen-baskets out in the pantry and yawned. I drew some pictures on my order-pad – small sketches of a pantryman, a row of glasses, a stack of silver trays, a bus boy counting napkins. Mespoulets had a rubber band, which, with two fingers of each hand, he stretched into various geometric shapes. He was impressed by my drawings.

The second night the dining-room was half full, but not a single guest sat at our tables. Mespoulets pulled at my serving napkin and whispered, 'If I were you, if I had your talent, that is what I would do,' and then he waved his napkin towards the centre of the room.

There a small group of the best guests of the Splendide sat at dinner. He waved his napkin at Table No. 18, where a man was sitting with a very beautiful woman. Mespoulets explained to me that this gentleman was a famous cartoonist, that he drew pictures of a big and a little man. The big man always hit the little man on the head. In this simple fashion the creator of those two figures made a lot of money.

We left our tables to go down and look at him. While I stood off to one side, Mespoulets circled around the table and cleaned the cartoonist's ashtray so that he could see whether or not the lady's jewellery was genuine. 'Yes, that's what I would do if I had your talent. Why do you want to be an actor? It's almost as bad as being a waiter,' he said when we returned to our station. We walked down again later on. This time Mespoulets spoke to the waiter who served Table No. 18, a Frenchman named Herriot, and asked what kind of guest the cartoonist was. Was he liberal?

'*Ah*,' said Herriot, '*c'ui là? Ah, oui alors! C'est un très bon client, extrêmement généreux. C'est un gentleman par excellence*.' And in English he added, 'He's A-1, that one. If only they were all like him! Never looks at the bill, never complains – and so full of jokes! It is a pleasure to serve him. *C'est un chic type*.'

After the famous cartoonist got his change, Herriot stood by waiting for the tip, and Mespoulets cruised around the table.

Herriot quickly snatched up the tip; both waiters examined it, and then Mespoulets climbed back to the balcony. '*Magnifique*,' he said to me. 'You are an idiot if you do not become a cartoonist. I am an old man—I have sixty years. All my children are dead, all except my daughter Mélanie, and for me it is too late for anything. I will always be a waiter. But you – you are young, you are a boy, you have talent. We shall see what can be done with it.'

Mespoulets investigated the famous cartoonist as if he were going to make him a loan or marry his daughter off to him. He interviewed chambermaids, telephone operators, and room waiters. 'I hear the same thing from the rest of the hotel,' he reported on the third rainy day. 'He lives here at the hotel, he has a suite, he is married to a countess, he owns a Rolls-Royce. He gives wonderful parties, eats grouse out of season, drinks vintage champagne at ten in the morning. He spends half the year in Paris and has a place in the south of France. When the accounting department is stuck with a charge they've forgotten to put on somebody's bill they just put it on his. He never looks at them.'

'Break it up, break it up. Sh-h-h. Quiet,' said Monsieur Maxim, the *maître d'hôtel* on our station.

Mespoulets and I retired into the pantry, where we could talk more freely.

'It's a very agreeable life, this cartoonist life,' Mespoulets continued, stretching his rubber band. 'I would never counsel you to be an actor or an artist-painter. But a cartoonist, that is different. Think what fun you can have. All you do is think of amusing things, make pictures with pen and ink, have a big man hit a little man on the head, and write a few words over it. And I know you can do this easily. You are made for it.'

That afternoon, between luncheon and dinner, we went out to find a place where cartooning was taught. As we marched along Madison Avenue, Mespoulets noticed a man walking in front of us. He had flat feet and he walked painfully, like a skier going uphill.

Mespoulets said 'Pst,' and the man turned around. They recognised each other and promptly said, '*Ah, bonjour.*'

'You see?' Mespoulets said to me when we had turned into a side street. 'A waiter. A dog. Call "Pst," click your tongue, snap your fingers, and they turn around even when they are out for a walk and say, "Yes sir, no sir, *bonjour Monsieurdame.*" Trained poodles! For God's sakes, don't stay a waiter! If you can't be a cartoonist, be a street-cleaner, a dish-washer, anything. But don't be an actor or a waiter. It's the most awful occupation in the world. The abuse I have taken, the long hours, the smoke and dust in my lungs and eyes, and the complaints—*ah, c'est la barbe, ce métier.* My boy, profit by my experience. Take it very seriously, this cartooning.'

For months one does not meet anybody on the street with his neck in an aluminium-and-leather collar such as is worn in cases of ambulatory cervical fractures, and then in a single day one sees three of them. Or one hears Mount Chimborazo mentioned five times. This day was a flat-foot day. Mespoulets, like the waiter we met on Madison Avenue, had flat feet. And so did the teacher in the Andrea del Sarto Art Academy. Before this man had finished interviewing me, Mespoulets whispered in my ear, 'Looks and talks like a waiter. Let's get out of here.'

On our way back to the hotel we bought a book on cartooning, a drawing-board, pens and a pen-holder, and several soft pencils. On the first page of the book we read that before one could cartoon or make caricatures, one must be able to draw a face – a man, a woman – from nature. That was very simple, said Mespoulets. We had lots of time and the Splendide was filled with models. Two days later he bought another book on art and we visited the Metropolitan Museum. We bought all the newspapers that had comic strips. And the next week Mespoulets looked around, and everywhere among the guests he saw funny people. He continued to read to me from the book on how to become a cartoonist.

The book said keep a number of sharpened, very soft pencils handy for your work. I did, and for a while I was almost the only waiter who had a pencil when a guest asked for one. 'And remember,' said the book, 'you can never be expert in caricaturing people unless you shake off the fear of drawing people.' I tried to shake off the fear.

'Most people like to have their own pictures drawn,' Mespoulets read solemnly. 'Regular-featured people should be avoided, as they are too simple to draw. Your attention should be concentrated on the faces with unique features.'

The most 'unique' faces at the Splendide belonged to Monsieur and Madame Lawrance Potter Dreyspool. Madame Dreyspool was very rich; her husband was not. He travelled with her as a sort of companion-butler, pulling her chair, helping her to get up, carrying books, flasks, dog-leashes, small purchases, and opera-glasses. He was also like the attendant at a sideshow, for Madame was a monstrosity and everyone stared at her. They were both very fat, but she was enormous. It was said that she got her clothes from a couturier specialising in costumes for women who were *enceinte*, and that to pull everything in shape and get into her dresses she had to lie down on the floor. She was fond of light pastel-coloured fabrics, and her ensembles had the colours of pigeons, hyacinths, and boudoir upholstery. Her coat covered her shoes and a wide fur piece her neck, and even in the middle of winter she wore immense garden hats that were as elaborate as wedding cakes.

Monsieur and Madame Dreyspool were the terror of *maîtres d'hôtel* all over the world. Wherever they stayed, they had the table nearest the entrance to the dining-room. This table was reserved for them at the Splendide in New York, at Claridge's in London, at the Ritz in Paris, and in various restaurants on the luxurious boats on which they crossed. Like the first snow-flakes, Monsieur and Madame Dreyspool always appeared in the Splendide at the beginning of the season. They left for Palm Beach at the first sign of its end.

Their entrance into the dining-room was spectacular. First Madame waddled in, then Monsieur with a Pekingese, one of the few dogs allowed in the main dining-room. Madame answered with one painful nod Monsieur Victor's deep bow, climbed up the two steps to the balcony on the right, where their table was, and elaborately sat down. Everyone in society knew them and nodded, coming in and going out. Monsieur and Madame thanked them briefly from the throne. They never spoke to each other and they never smiled.

Monsieur Dreyspool had consoled himself with whisky so many years that his face was purple. The gossip in the couriers' dining-room, where the valets and maids and chauffeurs ate, was that he also consoled himself with Susanne, Madame's personal maid. He did not seem so fat when he was alone, but when he and Madame were sitting together at their table on the good balcony, they looked like two old toads on a lily leaf.

The *maître d'hôtel* who took care of them was a Belgian and had come from the Hôtel de Londres in Antwerp. He never took his eyes off their table, and raced to it whenever Monsieur Dreyspool turned his head. Monsieur and Madame were waited upon by a patient old Italian waiter named Giuseppe. Because he never lost his temper and never made mistakes, he got all the terrible guests, most of whom paid him badly. Madame Dreyspool was not allowed any sugar. Her vegetables had to be cooked in a special fashion. A long letter of instruction about her various peculiarities hung in the offices of the chefs and *maîtres d'hôtel* of all the hotels she went to. It was mailed ahead to the various managers by Monsieur.

The exit of Monsieur and Madame Dreyspool was as festive as the entrance. When they were ready to leave, the *maître d'hôtel* pulled Monsieur's chair out. Monsieur pulled out Madame's chair. Madame produced the dog from her generous lap – it had slept there under a fold of the table-cloth while she ate – and gave the dog to Monsieur, who placed it on the carpet. Then the *maître d'hôtel*, taking steps as small as Madame's, escorted her out, walking on her left side and talking to her solicitously, his face close to hers. Monsieur followed about six feet behind, with a big Belinda Fancy Tales cigar between his teeth, his hands in his pockets, and the leash of the dog slipped over one wrist. From where Mespoulets and I stood on the bad balcony, she looked like several pieces of comfortable furniture piled together under a velvet cover and being slowly pushed along on little wheels.

Mespoulets was convinced that Madame Dreyspool was the very best possible model for me to begin drawing. The book said not to be afraid. 'Take a piece of paper,' it said, 'draw a line down the centre, divide this line, and draw another from left to right so that the paper is divided into four equal parts.' I took an old menu and stood on the good balcony between a screen and a marble column. It was possible there to observe and sketch Madame Dreyspool unnoticed. I divided the back of the menu into four equal parts. Once I started to draw, I saw that Madame's left half-face extended farther out from the nose than her right and that one eye was always half closed. When someone she knew came in, the eyelid went up over the rim of the pupil in greeting and the corners of the lips gave a short upward jump and then sank down again into a steady mask of disgust.

Monsieur and Madame were easy to draw, they hardly moved. They sat and stared – stared, ate, stared, stirred their coffee. Only their eyes moved, when Giuseppe brought the cheese or the pastry tray. Quickly, shiftily, they glanced over it, as one looks at something distasteful or dubious. Always the same sideways glance at the check, at Giuseppe when he took the tip, at the Belgian *maître d'hôtel*, and at Monsieur Victor as they left.

I took my sketches back to Mespoulets, who had been study-ing the book on art in the linen-closet. 'It shows effort and talent,' he said. 'It is not very good, but it is not bad. It is too stiff – looks too much like pigs, and while there is much pig at that table, it is marvellously complicated pig.' He considered the book a moment and then slapped it shut. 'I think,' he said, 'I understand the gist of art without reading any more of this. Try and be free of the helping lines. Tomorrow, when they come again, think of the kidney trouble, of the thousand *pâtés* and sauces they have eaten. Imagine those knees, the knees of Madame under the table – they must be so fat that faces are on each knee – two faces, one on each knee, laughing and frowning as she walks along. All that must be in the portrait. And the ankles that spill over her shoes – this must be evident in your drawing of her face.'

Monsieur and Madame came again the next day, and I stood under a palm and drew them on the back of another menu. Mespoulets came and watched me, broke a roll in half, and kneaded the soft part of the bread into an eraser. 'Much better,' he said. 'Try and try again. Don't give up. Remember the thousand fat sauces, the ankles. The eyes already are wonderful. Go ahead.'

He went back to his station, and soon after I heard 'Tsk, tsk, tsk, tsk!' over my shoulder. It was the Belgian *maître d'hôtel* and he was terror-stricken. He took the menu out of my hand and disappeared with it.

When I came to work the next noon I was told to report to the office of Monsieur Victor. I went to Monsieur Victor's desk. Slowly, precisely, without looking up from his list of reservations, he said, 'Ah, the *Wunderkind*.' Then, in the manner in which he discharged people, he continued, 'You are a talented young man. If I were you, I would most certainly become an artist. I think you should give all your time to it.' He looked up, lifted the top of his desk, and took out the portrait of Monsieur and Madame Lawrance Potter Dreyspool. 'As your first client, I would like to order four of these from you,' he said. 'Nicely done, like this one, but on good paper. If possible with some colour – green and blue and purple. And don't forget Monsieur's nose – the strawberry effect, the little blue veins – or the bags under the eyes. That will be very nice. A souvenir for my colleagues in London, Paris, Nice, and one for the *maître d'hôtel* on the *Mauretania*. You can have the rest of the day off to start on them.'

The Lost Mandolin

Towards the end of luncheon one day, as the orchestra was hurrying through its last number, 'Who Stole My Heart Away?', Mrs Lucius Le Grand Prideaux came up the steps of the main dining-room. She was one of the best clients of the Hotel Splendide, well connected, often photographed, and not only in society, but of it – a distinction which Monsieur Victor stressed in seating his clients.

Besides, she was beautiful and of such benevolent disposition that once when she broke open a roll and found a half-smoked cigar inside it, she did not complain or ask for the *maître d'hôtel*, but whispered to her waiter, Fenile, please to take it away. The cigar went downstairs to the Greek who feeds the plates into the dish-washing machine, and he retrieved it from among leftover green peas, celery stalks, and chicken bones. He wiped it dry and finished smoking it on the way home.

Fenile was duly grateful for this smooth settlement of the cigar butt. While he could not have been expected to see inside the roll, and the baker would eventually have been blamed, the first wrath of the *maître d'hôtel* always falls on the waiter.

Fenile was in love with Mrs Prideaux. He took every opportunity when serving her to brush his cheek against the feathers on her hat, his hand on her fur pieces and her clothes. He watched for the moment when she sat down, and unfolded the napkin and placed it on her lap himself. He brought her a footstool, although she never asked for one, and if she but turned her head, she saw him rushing to her side.

As Monsieur Victor showed her to a table now, she told him that the night before, at a costume party for charity given in the ballroom of the hotel, she had lost, or rather forgotten, a mandolin. She had come to the party as an Italian street singer. The mandolin was part of her costume and of no value; she had made it herself out of an old cigar-box and some odds and ends. If it was found, she would like to have it for sentimental reasons; if not, it was of no importance. As Monsieur Victor pulled Madame's chair and clicked his tongue for the captain who took care of her table, he promised that he would have the mandolin back in a few minutes.

Fenile came up with the napkin and climbed under the table with the footstool; the captain bent low to take her order, and Monsieur Victor left the table.

As always when removing himself from an important client, Monsieur Victor did a small ballet – he backed away, making three deep bows. The last bow bowed, he quickly turned and made a smaller fourth bow towards the table to which he had turned his back, and whispered, '*Pardon.*' Then he hurried with small steps to his desk at the door, his hands tense, as if life itself depended on the finding of the mandolin of Mrs Lucius Le Grand Prideaux. First he telephoned in person to von Kyling, the banquet manager, who ranked slightly below him. Von Kyling said that no musical instrument had been found. In a few minutes his assistant came running down to the restaurant and reported that nothing resembling a cigar-box or a mandolin had been left behind the night before, and that it was not among the lost and found articles listed on the report of the assistant banquet manager who had closed up. He added that they would immediately investigate.

Von Kyling himself came down shortly afterwards and reported that one of the housemen had seen a waiter pick up something out of a heap of confetti and broken glasses that was swept together in a corner of the ballroom – something that looked like a cigar-box. The man had thought at the time that it was just an empty, thrown-away cigar-box, but since he had heard that the mandolin was made out of a cigar-box, he thought he remembered some strings and a neck on it. In fact he was sure the waiter, as he took the object away, plucked the strings and made some sort of sound with it. Monsieur Victor asked what time the houseman had observed this. Right after he came on duty, von Kyling said, between seven and seven-thirty. Monsieur Victor dismissed the banquet manager with a nod of the head and called for his assistant. He asked him to get hold of the waiter who opened the breakfast-room, who must be the one that the houseman had seen.

The waiter who opened the breakfast-room at six-thirty every morning was a man by the name of Marvel, a Swiss. As soon as he came on duty he opened the windows, to ventilate the room, and then, with the help of a bus boy, took the chairs down off the tables, where they stood during the night so that the cleaners could get at the carpet with the vacuum machines. When Marvel had covered the tables with linen, the bus boy ran down for the boxes of silver, and together they put glasses, plates, and napkins around. This was followed with salt and pepper shakers, sugar, menus, and vases with flowers. Then the bus boy went down to get some coffee and rolls and butter, and before he filled the ice-water bottles, he and the waiter had their breakfast out in the pantry.

A captain later had his coffee and rolls behind a screen in the breakfast-room and read the newspapers until the first guests arrived. The name of the captain on breakfast duty was Guggenheim. His first name was Isidor, but since it was not in accord with the elegance of the Splendide to have a captain named Isidor, he was called Igor. Monsieur Igor was supposed to be at his post at seven, but he arrived as late as nine. He was hidden away in the breakfast-room and assigned to this unpleasant post because of his race. Marvel was there, too, away from the grandeur of the main restaurant, because he had a bad foot.

Marvel was a mouse of a waiter, jittery and scared. He could not speak without nervous pauses, and his right foot had been broken, and then badly set several times, after he had fallen down the iron stairs from the hotel pantry to the kitchen. He hid this defect as well as he could while he was in the hotel – he stood still in back of sideboards or screens, and when he went to a table or anywhere else, he ran. To anyone who did not know about his affliction he seemed to be in high spirits – hop, skip, hop, he danced along, the deep carpet swallowing the uneven gait. Out in the pantry, the tiled floor gave him away. On the street, when he left the hotel, he let himself go. He seemed to shift gears – the pivot changed, his body from the hips up seemed to rotate as he walked. The head bobbed up and down violently. The right foot was thrown down at the pavement in an angry, sudden slap – the way German soldiers march on parade. The left foot walked along quietly.

In the twenty years that Marvel had been in the service of the Splendide, he had learned no more English than was necessary to carry on his breakfast and luncheon conversations with guests, and even that was faulty. For example, he pronounced oatmeal as if it were the French for 'high honey' – '*haut miel*'. He knew his address and a few phrases. For the rest, he spoke only French and a Swiss-German dialect.

When Monsieur Victor sent for him, he was told that Marvel had, as usual, gone home for the afternoon. Guggenheim was up in the captain's dressing-room. Monsieur Victor told his assistant to call up the waiter and have him come immediately. Then he returned to the dining-room and reported to Mrs Prideaux that the search was progressing. She finished her lunch and left, telling Monsieur Victor not to go to too much trouble; the mandolin was of no great importance. Marvel had no telephone, and so the chief bus boy was sent to fetch him from his house, a few blocks away on First Avenue.

At four o'clock Monsieur Victor got together everyone who had anything to do with the closing of the ballroom and the opening of the breakfast-room. There were about a dozen employees gathered in the empty breakfast-room. Monsieur Victor had the talents of a district attorney. The assistant *maître d'hôtel* put a chair between two tall vases of hydrangeas, the doors were closed, and Monsieur Victor sat down. Marvel was the first to be questioned.

'You are the breakfast waiter?'

'*Oui*, M'sieur Victor.'

'You are on duty in the breakfast-room from six o'clock on?'

'*Oui*, M'sieur Victor.'

'And your duty is mainly to stay in that room and wait for the first guest?'

'*Oui*, M'sieur Victor.'

'But apparently you don't, Marvel. You make excursions, Marvel. You run all over the house.' Monsieur Victor looked at Marvel's foot. 'What business, Marvel, have you in the ballroom, hmm?'

'No business, M'sieur Victor.'

'You were seen in the ballroom this morning at seven, picking up a mandolin. The houseman there saw you.' Monsieur Victor turned to the houseman. 'This is the man, isn't it?'

'*Si*, Signor Victor, that's him.'

Monsieur Victor turned back to Marvel. 'Where is that mandolin, Marvel?'

'I took it home, M'sieur Victor.'

'You took it home – he took it home! *Da hört sich doch alles auf*,' said Monsieur Victor to Guggenheim, with whom he usually spoke in German. 'You took it home. Do you know the rules of this hotel, Marvel? Do you know that you are never to take anything out of the house, even your own belongings, without a written permission from your department head? Do you know that all things that are found must be turned over to the office?'

'*Oui*, M'sieur Victor.'

'Then why did you take that mandolin home?'

'Because, M'sieur Victor, because it was junk – it lay in a pile of dust and confetti and sweepings and torn paper hats.

It was just a cigar-box and I wanted it to take home to my little boy.'

'Run home, Marvel, and bring back that mandolin immediately!'

'M'sieur Victor—'

Monsieur Victor seemed surprised that Marvel still stood there. He turned his head in a listening gesture and said, 'Yes?'

'He broke the mandolin, my little boy. But it was already no good when I took it home. Somebody must have stepped on it while cleaning up and sweeping – maybe one of the housemen.'

Monsieur Victor looked at the houseman, who shook his head. 'Go home and bring back the mandolin,' Monsieur Victor said, white with anger. 'Don't give me any more explanations. Go home and bring it as it is, in pieces, but bring it and hurry up.'

Marvel danced out of the room and pounded down the stairs.

Monsieur Victor told his assistant to go and call Madame Prideaux and tell her that he hoped to return the mandolin the next day. Then he turned to the others and asked why this mandolin had not been found by Maurice, the assistant banquet manager, when he closed up at 4 a.m. And why did Monsieur Igor, the breakfast captain, not see to it that his waiters stayed where they belonged, in the breakfast-room, instead of running all over the hotel, hmmm?

'Heads are going to roll,' the chief bus boy said as he came out of the examination. 'Wait and see.'

Marvel came back with the broken mandolin as the waiters began setting the main dining-room for dinner. He ran to Monsieur Victor's desk, unwrapped the mandolin, and showed it to him. The neck had come loose from the cigar-box body – the strings alone held it together – and the side of the box was splintered. Marvel's face looked like wet putty.

Monsieur Victor told Marvel to take it up to the carpenter shop and have it repaired and to find out what it cost, and then to report back to him.

Marvel took the elevator up to the roof of the hotel, where the carpenter shop was, and when he came back he reported that it would be fixed by the next morning, and that there was no charge. Monsieur Victor picked up the telephone and called the carpenter shop. The head carpenter, a Frenchman, told him it was a bagatelle; he did not see how he could charge for it. All it needed was a little glue; he would press it overnight, varnish it in the morning, let it dry, and it would be better looking than it had ever been.

'I want you to charge for it,' said Monsieur Victor, 'just to teach this waiter a lesson. I want you to charge five dollars for repairing this mandolin on the Splendide's time, with the Splendide's materials. I will have him pay it here at the cashier's desk.'

He put down the telephone and turned to Marvel. 'Have you five dollars, Marvel?' Marvel went through all his pockets, but he could not find more than a dollar and sixty cents. Monsieur Victor gave him a slip of paper to sign – an order to deduct the sum of five dollars from his pay – and then he turned to him, pursing his lips as if he were about to kiss him. 'And now, Marvel, get out of here,' he said. 'Turn in your apron and your check-book and your locker key. You are discharged.'

Marvel looked at Victor as if he had never seen him before. *'Espèce d'un salaud! Du Hund – du – du – du Lump, du Sauhaufen!'* he stuttered. 'You dirty, filthy dog!' – and then he kicked Victor hard with the bad foot, and ran with surprising agility – humpty dump – out of the dining-room towards the ballroom. Monsieur Victor ran after him.

Marvel took the steps three at a time and disappeared into the ballroom. The room was darkened, and in it stood some scaffolding that had been used to stage the pageant of the charity ball the night before. Marvel, having been there that morning, knew where it was, but Monsieur Victor, who never stayed for a charity affair, did not. Marvel ducked and ran to the exit that led to a service stairway and down to the waiters' locker-room. But Monsieur Victor ran head on into the scaffolding. He fell, dislocated an ankle, lost two teeth, and had to be carried back to his office.

In his office, Monsieur Victor lay on a couch, moaned and cursed, and held a handkerchief to his mouth. Presently he grew calmer and called his assistant to his side, as if this were his deathbed. He instructed him in a gasping and muffled tone to telephone Mrs Prideaux again that the mandolin had been recovered.

Then Monsieur Victor allowed himself to be taken home.

It was the first time that the *maître d'hôtel* of the Splendide had been absent. It seemed impossible that the hotel could run without him, but it did. An assistant *maître d'hôtel* was at the door, and collected nice tips. The air was freer, the music seemed more lively. When the guests asked where Monsieur Victor was, they were told that he was indisposed. The waiters outside in the pantry stood in groups, laughing and pushing up their upper lips, to show those who did not know which two of Monsieur Victor's teeth had been knocked out. Others went up to visit the scene of the accident. The pantryman showed how Monsieur Victor had limped and groaned. Everybody was very happy about it. Marvel, who had left the hotel as soon as he was dressed, stood outside the employees' entrance in a circle of admirers. He was patted on the back and congratulated, and later he stamped home. Only the lady cashiers and the captains professed concern. The house doctor was sent to Monsieur Victor, and everyone waited for bulletins from the bedside.

A lot of letters and orders to be signed had piled up. The chef had prepared a bottle of double strength *consommé volaille* to be sent to Monsieur Victor, to aid his recovery, and I was chosen to go to his house with it, and to have the papers signed. I carried also a letter from the *maîtres d'hôtel* expressing their sympathies and hopes for quick convalescence. The lady cashiers sent a bouquet of flowers.

Monsieur Victor lived in a brownstone house on East Forty-eighth Street. He occupied an apartment on the first floor, three rooms, of which the living-room was towards the rear of the building. A woman who must have been his wife led me back to it, took the *consommé*, and disappeared through a sliding door. The room consisted of four high walls, broken by the high, thick frames of doors and windows. It was papered in brown. A few pieces of furniture stood on a dark carpet – furniture such as one sees in rooming-houses and auction rooms – two large chairs, a couch, a table with a velvet cover edged with pompons. Over a cast-iron fireplace, in a mahogany frame, hung a picture of two people praying in a field. Everything in the room was somehow related in colour to the wilted flat sienna colour of the wallpaper, and the only bright object that caught light was a glass-and-brass canary cage, hung near the window, with a leaf of lettuce stuck through the bars. A rubber plant, a foot and a half high, stood in a porcelain pot in the centre of the window-sill.

Monsieur Victor was almost unrecognisable without his tailcoat, high collar, and tie. He was unshaven, and he was wearing a flannel bathrobe with Indian designs on it. His lips were swollen, one eye was discoloured, and he had his right foot in a tub of hot water. On his head was a helmet of cardboard, and from it a wire led up to the chandelier, a brass instrument with two elaborate arms. On each arm was a glass bowl, with a lighted bulb in one and the electric cord from the helmet attached to the other.

This apparatus, he explained to me, was for restoring hair. He was not yet bald, but the hair was thinning in two spots above his forehead. He rubbed a black salve into his scalp, he told me, and then put on the hat. Inside the hat burned a blue electric lamp – a quartz light, he said it was – and it was supposed to make hair grow. He took off the hat and showed me a film of fine new hair such as women have on their cheeks.

Monsieur Victor did not mention the accident. He read the captains' letters, signed some papers, and said that it was high time to put some discipline into the restaurant and the ballroom. 'Their goose honks too high,' he said. He advised me to remember to fire somebody at least every six months – whether they did anything bad or not. It keeps the rest on their toes, he said.

He reproached himself for not having fired Marvel sooner – he also regretted not having got rid of Guggenheim. 'A Jew for a *maître d'hôtel* and a cripple for a waiter,' he moaned. And then he reflected on the fact that both of them had been with the hotel since it opened. He said, 'The boast of some places that their employees have been with them such a very long time – and this is something to remember also – is entirely idiotic. Most people have simply not been found out. The fact that an employee has been with you twenty years might only mean that for twenty years he has got away with something, he has become a fixture – his faults have been overlooked – he gets more and more lazy. Old employees are dangerous to have around. There comes a time when you can't fire them any more. Besides, the fact that these two have been nothing but waiter and captain for twenty years, without trying to

improve themselves or looking for another job, shows, in itself
that they are incompetent. Out with them!'

He rubbed some new grease on his head, put on his electric hat again, and told me that he had ordered the discharge
of Guggenheim. He had also ordered the discharge of the
assistant banquet manager. 'Now we come to the captains,' he
said. 'I'll make them toe the line from now on. Captains, ah!
Maîtres d'hôtel they call themselves – a bunch of shoemakers –
dumm, faul, und gefrässig! Write,' he said. 'Start with capital
letters – "MESSIEURS LES CAPITAINES" – put a line under
that' – and then he dictated the following:

MESSIEURS LES CAPITAINES

*Chaque capitaine sera tenu responsable du service de sa station,
c'est à dire: de la mise en place, de la bonne conduite des garçons
de commis sous ses ordres. Chaque capitaine sera également
tenu responsable de l'amabilité, et de la politesse des garçons,
et du bon service rendu à tous les clients (sans exception). La
direction tiendra strict compte de toutes les plaintes des clients,
et agira en conséquence.*

*Il est absolument défendu d'avoir des discussions, ou des
conversations inutiles dans la salle.*

La place de chaque capitaine est: à sa station.

*Le capitaine du 'Breakfast' doit être dans la salle à six heures
le matin. Tous les capitaines doivent être dans la salle à midi 30
et à 6 h. 30 du soir. Les capitaines de garde l'après-midi doivent*

être dans la salle, le lendemain matin, l'un à 11 h. 30 et l'autre à midi (à tour de rôle), et tous les deux à 5 h. 30 du soir.

Un des capitaines de garde de l'après-midi (à tour de rôle) doit s'occuper, tout spécialement, du transport des tables et des chaises du Restaurant, et ce capitaine sera responsable du bon état du matériel ainsi transporté. Ces messieurs seront tenus responsables de ce qu'il y ait toujours deux garçons et deux commis de garde dans la salle après le déjeuner, jusqu'à ce que ceux-ci soient remplacés par les premiers qui remonteront de leur déjeuner.

Le capitaine de garde le soir sera tenu responsable du service en général de toute la salle. Il devra voir à ce qu'il y ait toujours des cartes de souper, et que seulement celles-ci *soient présentées aux clients. Il devra voir également à ce que les garçons ne se servent que des 'Check-books' des soupers du Restaurant.*

Tous ces messieurs les capitaines (sans exception) doivent entrer, et sortir, par le 'Timekeeper', et faire timbrer leur carte.

Each captain shall be held responsible for the service at his post, viz.: for setting up, and for the good conduct of the commis waiters under his orders. Each captain shall also be held responsible for his waiters' polite good humour, and for the quality of the service provided to each and every client (without exception). The hotel's management will take rigorous account of any and all complaints received from its clients, and will *act accordingly*.

Unnecessary discussions or conversations in the dining-room are strictly forbidden.

Each captain's place is: *at his post*.

The breakfast-room captain must be on duty at 6 a.m. sharp. All captains must be present in the dining-room by 12.30 p.m. and 6.30 p.m. The duty captains for the afternoon service shall be present in the dining-room the following morning: one at 11.30 a.m. and the other at noon (by turns). Both shall be present from 5.30 p.m. onwards.

One afternoon duty captain in turn shall be responsible for the transfer of the Restaurant tables and chairs, and the same shall be held responsible for the good condition of the items transferred. The same gentleman shall ensure that two waiters and two duty commis waiters are present in the dining-room after luncheon, at all times, until they are relieved of their posts by the waiters of the first service on return their midday meal in the pantry.

The late-evening duty captain shall be held responsible for the service as a whole, in the dining-room as a whole. He must ensure that supper menus are always available, and that *these and no others* are presented to the clients. He shall furthermore ensure that the waiters use *only* the check-books reserved for supper in the Restaurant.

All gentlemen captains must enter and leave via the 'Timekeeper' and ensure their time-card is stamped.

The last part of the manifesto irked the *maîtres d'hôtel* the most. Up to now they had been allowed to enter the hotel through the doors that were used by the guests.

The woman who must have been his wife came in, scarcely visible in the dark room. She had warmed the *consommé* and brought two cups, bread, salt, and napkins. Following her, a child came into the room—a wobbly infant with a large head and pale eyes. It looked like Monsieur Victor and had his arrogant mouth – a little *maître d'hôtel* with a dribbly lip. He came close to me and examined me – he drank me in with ears, nose, and open mouth, and then he pulled at my trousers and made a few sounds.

'My son,' said Monsieur Victor, and he smiled with pride.

He had taken off the electric hat and it lay on its side on the floor, the blue lamp, still lighted, throwing a beam from the cardboard cone. With my fingers I made some shadow figures on the wall – a rabbit, a crocodile, and a face that opened and closed its mouth. Both father and son were amused.

Victor *père* looked at me searchingly for an instant, and then settled back comfortably in his pillows. 'You may go,' he said after a short silence, and I stuffed the papers into my coat pocket and left.

IV

Easy Money

On one of the upper floors of the Hotel Splendide was a private dining-room large enough for a horseshoe table on which covers for sixty people could be laid; with the aid of folding doors, it could be made small enough to accommodate a group of four in intimate comfort. This suite had its own serving-pantry and its own complete kitchen. A chef, his assistants, scullery help, and a pantryman had to be there for even the simplest dinners.

The staff which served there – the *maître d'hôtel*, the captains, the bar-tenders, the footmen – were chosen by the banquet department for their tact and good presence and because they were able to work all night long and be as awake at five in the morning as they had been at nine the night before.

The suite was frequently used for gay dinners and for instantaneous courtships. It was also engaged for the discussion of serious affairs. Men important in business or with positions of responsibility in Washington met here, and in the course of an evening a violent change often came on them. They arrived with dignity, and they looked important and like the photographs of them published in newspapers, but in the late hours they became Joe or Stewy or Lucius. Sometimes they fell on their faces and sang into the carpet. Leaders of the nation, savants, and unhappy millionaires suffered fits of laughter, babbled nonsense, and spilled ashes and wine down their shirt-fronts. Some of them became ill. Others swam in a happy haze and loved all the world.

On such a party, a drunken financier would throw one arm about a senator and hang the other arm around a judge's neck. Then the three would fall back onto a soft sofa. The financier would shout, 'Waiter! Hey, waiter – pencil and paper! Oh, where is that goddamned waiter?'

A waiter was nearly always right there, and he carried a pencil and a pad. On this pad he usually wrote his orders and, to facilitate service, he made a duplicate with a sheet of carbon paper, which he kept for himself in case of dispute.

When a guest asked for a piece of paper, the waiter handed him his pad. But first he moved the carbon, ordinarily under the first sheet of paper, a few sheets back and tucked it well out of sight. When the guest had written his note and had torn it off, the waiter took back his pad and went behind a screen or out into the pantry to see what the guest had written. The morality of this did not bother the waiters. The tender plant that is morality does not thrive in a grand hotel, and withers altogether in its private rooms. The information that they read was frequently of no value to them, but once in a while it turned out to be very profitable. The waiters were always hopeful. Sometimes, by means of the carbon paper in his pad, a waiter had access to information for which bankers and statesmen would have licked boots, and had it long before tense young men in Wall Street were rushing around with it.

If the party lasted long enough, it was not necessary to bother with the carbon paper in the pad. While certain of the guests were starting to make trouble and breaking things, there was always at least one who backed the *maître d'hôtel*, a favourite waiter, or the wine steward against the bar and said, 'Ambrose, I am going to make you rich!' Then he stood away and tried to bring the man's face in focus. 'Now listen, Ambrose,' he said, and both his hands came down on Ambrose's shoulders, like two hammers. Ambrose's knees gave way and he was pinned against the bar. While he was down, he tried to pick up his benefactor's cigar before it burned a hole in the rug. When he came up, the guest hung his weight on him and said, 'Ambrose, I told you I was going to make you rich, didn't I? Well, I will,' and hammered him again. Ambrose came up for the second time, and then, slowly, thoroughly, as if for an idiot, it was explained to him what stock to buy and when to sell.

In this fashion, working as an assistant *maître d'hôtel* in the banquet department, I became rich several times. It was not unusual, after a small dinner, for one of the waiters to make a thousand dollars or a bus boy five hundred.

Information got in this way was closely guarded. The serving staff of the private dining-room were used to making money, and they were not eager to share their privileges with the rank and file of the hotel staff. Only to von Kyling, the head of the banquet department, and to one or two close friends were they likely to impart what they knew. Nevertheless, such information occasionally leaked out. When a guest left one of these parties, the *maître d'hôtel* or a waiter would see him down the corridor, push the elevator button, and wait at a respectful distance. After the guest had entered the lift and laid his hat and cane on the seat, he sometimes came out again, told the elevator boy to wait, and for the tenth time repeated some piece of information to his friend. The elevator boy strained his ears, and next day the information was all over the hotel.

The Wall Street fever hit the banquet department hardest. The waiters who work for banquets are more bohemian than regular waiters. They dislike steady employment and they are migratory workers. They are in Palm Beach and

Havana after the New York season; they work in a club and play the horses in Saratoga during August; with the opening of the Metropolitan they are back in New York. They start and stop work at irregular hours and make irregular money. During the market boom it was hard to keep them working. But all the employees played the market, whether they had inside information or not. The conservative elements – cooks, chambermaids, *valets de chambre* – invested chiefly in shares of Cities Service. Even Monsieur Victor caught the fever.

Once a week, on Thursdays, a peculiar thin man, a Mr Tannenbaum, came to the main dining-room for luncheon wearing a dark, high-buttoned suit and cotton gloves, which he did not take off until he sat down. Monsieur Victor reserved the same table for him week after week. He was immediately given a stack of napkins and a second table was put close by. On this second table the waiter put several alcohol burners and lighted them.

After Mr Tannenbaum had tucked his gloves in his pocket, he took a napkin, opened it, and began to polish the silver on his table. He drew the cloth between the prongs of his fork, pulling it this way and that; then, with grimaces, he rubbed the knives and the spoons. Next, he wiped his water glass and the tumbler for his milk and looked through them, holding them up against the lighted chandelier. Last, he shined the plates. When all this was done he covered the glass with one napkin, the silver and the plates with another, and turned his attention to ordering.

The waiter whose misfortune it was to serve Mr Tannenbaum was the old, meek, unexcitable Italian, Giuseppe. He was always at his station half an hour before mealtime and always there until the last guest had gone. He never forgot anything, never broke a thing, spoke to few people, and left the room only for a quick glance at the market quotations in the afternoon papers. Of all the waiters in the restaurant, Giuseppe was the only one capable of looking after Mr Tannenbaum.

Mr Tannenbaum lived on a strict diet of cereals, boiled rice, celery, stewed fruits, and milk. His food was brought steaming to the side table and put over the alcohol flames before it was allowed to cool. His butter was brought in a special covered dish, his gluten bread wrapped in two napkins. All the time he was eating he watched for flies. His meals were almost a religious ceremony. Lights burned, silver shone, vessels were covered and uncovered or moved from one side of the table to the other. The ceremonial of the washing of the hands took place before he ate his compote of stewed fruit. Silent prayers were said by Giuseppe lest something go wrong and he be discharged. To this atmosphere of *Te Deum* and fetish, the ascetic countenance of Mr Tannenbaum was entirely appropriate. It was the face of a man a few days drowned, his hair the colour of ashes.

At the end of the meal he added up the bill and frequently disputed prices; they were always adjusted in his favour. From the inside pocket of his coat he drew a fresh pair of white cotton gloves. When he had put them on he carefully arranged the coins he had received in change and gave Giuseppe the smallest possible tip. He never gave anything to the captain or to Monsieur Victor. Nevertheless, Monsieur Victor watched over him as over a sick horse. He hovered about Mr Tannenbaum's table from the moment he was seated until he left the restaurant. The reason for his solicitude over this aseptic guest was that Mr Tannenbaum had charge of investing the funds of a great university and of several large charitable organisations, as well as the fortunes of a few people who were almost God.

Monsieur Victor played the market on the information from the private parties; but occasionally, when Wall Street seemed too wild, he took a cab down to the financial district and was admitted to Mr Tannenbaum's office. So sage was the advice he received there that in the late fall of 1929, when we read of a great many of our guests jumping out of windows and a great many others were beginning to talk to themselves in the street, Monsieur Victor rubbed his hands together with joy, was debonair with his guests and employees, and thought of building himself a villa on the Riviera.

Giuseppe, though, never received a word of advice from Mr Tannenbaum, the most difficult of all his guests. Giuseppe owned a little house somewhere in Queens – one of a thousand exactly alike. In that house lived his Italian mother, his wife, and his two sons. Giuseppe had sent both boys to college, one to study architecture, the other medicine. Now that they were through school the old waiter felt his worst troubles were over, and he wanted to invest his earnings.

One of his guests, an official of the National City Bank, advised him to buy all the stock of that bank he could carry. Giuseppe did, and made money on it. A steel man who lunched at one of his tables told him to sell his National City Bank stock and buy U.S. Steel. He made more in that stock. His third piece of advice came from a woman who had persuaded her husband to employ Giuseppe's architect son. She told Giuseppe to invest in Postum the profits he had made in National City Bank and in U.S. Steel. Giuseppe followed her advice and it worked out quite well.

Naturally, the stock market interfered with the service of the Hotel Splendide. Waiters stood in line trying to get at a telephone to call their brokers. In the restaurant they collected in groups, where they discussed trends, exchanged market tips and advice, and shouted quotations at each other. They calculated profits on the backs of menus and they disappeared for long stretches of time, during which they sat in some out-of-the-way corner of the hotel, dreaming and planning what to do with their profits. Whenever the market was bullish, they became wild-eyed and nervous. A few hundred dollars to the good, they whistled in the pantry and ran up and down the stairs that led to the kitchen. At such times complaints from the guests increased tenfold. When someone asked a waiter why he had to wait so long for a slice of lemon for his fish, the waiter was quite likely to answer that he did not carry sliced lemons in his pockets, that he had to get them from the kitchen, and that he had only two legs and two arms.

One lovely day in June 1929, Giuseppe picked up a newspaper one of his guests had left behind, and in the middle of luncheon went out to look at the financial page. He did some mental calculation, and he saw that he was a free man with enough money to last him as long as he lived. When he came back he walked straight to Monsieur Victor, who was standing in the centre of the dining-room. First Giuseppe took off his apron, threw it on the floor, and stepped on it. Then he made a loud speech in which he told Monsieur Victor what he thought of him. After that he spat on the carpet in front of Monsieur Victor's shoes, pushed an assistant *maître d'hôtel* aside, and walked out.

Monsieur Victor was so upset that he had to remain in his office the rest of the afternoon. He seemed inches shorter than usual. One eye stared out into the foyer. Towards evening he told his secretary to make sure that all the *maîtres d'hôtel* in New York were informed of this disgraceful affair, so that if Giuseppe ever came to them looking for work, he would be dealt with properly. The next day Monsieur Victor paid a visit to Mr Tannenbaum. When he returned he said, 'Giuseppe will be back again – on his knees and crying for a job.'

He was right. In November Giuseppe came back, properly bent and broken, and as he stood before Monsieur Victor in the *maître d'hôtel*'s office, he let the rim of his hat run through his hands. Monsieur Victor looked at him from his necktie down to his shoes, omitting the face entirely. When Giuseppe was asked to explain his scandalous behaviour, he made helpless gestures with one hand, dropped his hat, and picked it up. Eventually he squeezed out an apology that was mostly inaudible. Monsieur Victor had to say to him several times, 'Speak louder, I can't hear what you're saying.' And after Giuseppe had finished, Monsieur Victor turned his head away and said, 'Mumbling won't help.'

Giuseppe went out into the pantry when the interview was over and suffered a crying spell. The waiters talked to him on their way to and from the dining-room, and later in the afternoon one of them went home with him.

Monsieur Victor let Giuseppe wait a week. Then, because Giuseppe had been with the hotel for a very long time, because he was a very good waiter, and because Mr Tannenbaum and the Dreyspools were asking for him and complaining about the man who had been put in his place, Monsieur Victor forgave him.

V

Kalakobé

There was only one Negro on the staff of the Hotel Splendide. Perhaps my fondness for Negroes is explained by the fact that when I was a child and lived in Munich and in Tirol, I saw Negroes only in rare, exciting, and happy moments.

The first one I met was a coloured baby, which arrived one day in the mail. It smiled from the cover of a small, hand-coloured booklet which was sent out by the secretariat of the

Munich Archbishop and requested a small donation towards the maintenance of a mission in Africa. The child, called *Negerlein* (the Bavarian diminutive of Negro), sat among lions and tigers and stretched its arms out to me.

The next time I saw Negroes was a year later in Munich, at the Circus Renz – an intimate circus, red, white, and gold, with only one ring about the size of the bottom of a merry-go-round. In this circus performed one clown, a small elephant, and an acrobatic rider who changed his clothes on a see-sawing white horse – he wore about fifteen different suits, and he peeled them off one after another, becoming in turn an admiral, a policeman, a travelling Englishman, and finally a Tirolean.

After this act came the Africans, billed as the Fierce Wassabi Tribe. Breaking into the ring with aboriginal noises, they did a tribal dance with bleached skulls, lances, and beautiful shields. They wore leopard skins, chains of gold, head-dresses of ostrich feathers. After the performance I was allowed to go back and visit them. They sat in an artificial palm-leaf village, their knees as high as their cheeks.

When the chief and his wife shook hands with me, I was somewhat disappointed to notice the pink palms of their hands. The chief allowed me, however, to wet my finger and try to rub some of the black from his knee, and when it did not come off I was proud to have met him and I was sure he was a real Negro. But nowhere on the street, in the parks, in the houses, or out in the fields and mountains were there any Negroes. You had to pay dearly to see them; they were expensive people, and never used for carrying luggage or running an elevator.

The Splendide's Negro was a Senegalese, and very black, and his name was Kalakobé. He had come to New York five years before and had found work in the kitchens of the hotel because he was a Frenchman. Besides French, he spoke an African dialect and a few words of English, and he always insisted that he was not a Negro but an African.

Kalakobé was employed under the magnificent title of 'casserolier', a job for which it was very difficult to find anyone. The casserolier had to drag huge casseroles across the floor, and copper and iron pots that were sometimes four feet and more in diameter, lift them into wooden tubs, wash them, and put them back where they belonged. This work took a man of immense strength, and therefore everybody was glad that Kalakobé was so big and that he worked ten hours a day year in, year out and sang while he was working. He had shoulders like two shovels. He stood in a steam-filled room, a pantry all his own, and here he knocked the huge pots around and poured streams of hot water from one into another. He was bare to the waist and worked under a strong light that made him blue-black, except when he was scrubbing the outside of the casseroles. Then his body was red wherever the copper reflected. As he lifted the largest of the casseroles, a play of muscles started on his back, cords pulled, ridges rose, like oxen dragging a weight. It was a lesson in anatomy.

If Kalakobé was not in his pantry, there were four places where he could be found: in the silver room, under the stairs of the Jade Suite, in the ballroom, or at the uniform tailor's shop.

Under the stairs of the Jade Suite he had built a small jungle. Someone had given him a broken-down couch, and he had hung up several carpets which were not in use; they formed the walls. In there he sat, ate, and sometimes slept by the light of candles.

He was at his most beautiful in the silver room.

After he was through scrubbing the casseroles that were used for cooking the midday meal for about eight hundred guests, he went to the room where the hotel silver was cleaned, and there he attended two Tahara machines, which are wooden drums that turn. Inside each drum are thousands of little pellets like bird-shot. The drum is opened, a quantity of silverware is put in, and with it a large piece of soap the colour of strawberry ice-cream. When the drum is closed and starts to turn, the pellets inside sound like the ocean far away. After a while the drum is opened, the silver is taken out, rinsed off, and dried. It is then as bright as new. The Hotel Splendide's silver passed through these machines almost constantly.

In this room Kalakobé stood against a background of champagne-coolers, soup tureens, rows of candelabra, trays, and dishes of every size. When these had been washed and dried, there were hundreds of forks, spoons, demitasse spoons, and silver knives for him to do. From all these objects a shimmering white light reflected, so that his body from the waist up was covered with silver scales. He had cut away from his shoes the part that covered his toes, and his trousers were held up with a red sash, and no matter where he stood, he was always a good portrait. The bare walls of the silver room were tiled, and against the precise divisions of the tiles one could measure him and even his movements – three tiles across for the shoulder, eight from the elbow to the wrist, and ten from the top of his head to the first ribs on his chest.

He was most happy in the workshop of the old tailor who made the uniforms for the hotel staff and pressed and repaired them. Kalakobé brought food to the tailor's cat and held it in his arms while he sat in a corner of the room, watching the doormen with envy as they were being measured for new coats. His dream was to be a doorman some day and wear a beautiful uniform. Occasionally he would get up and stand in front of the rows of closets in which gala liveries for footmen and elevator boys hung, or go through the drawers filled with epaulettes, gold and silver braid, crests, pale-blue silken knee breeches, fancy caps, and pumps with gilded buckles. When the tailor was not too busy, Kalakobé tried on various liveries. One day the tailor made him a present of a doorman's coat that was too far gone to be worn before the Splendide's elegant entrance, and Kalakobé was beside himself with gratitude. He put extra buttons and trimming on it, and then took it home with him, to use as a dressing-gown or bathrobe.

When Kalakobé was through working and ready to go home, he dressed with extreme care. His plum-coloured suit fitted his athletic frame like a sweater; his socks were the colour of a wet frog. Into a neon-red tie he sank the point of an imitation-gold tie-pin – a crocodile with paste rubies for eyes and four false emeralds for teeth. Out of his pocket he brought a lapis-lazuli ring and a golden one with an obscure African arrangement of two nude ladies beaten into it. Then he slipped on a form-fitting mauve overcoat that reached almost to the floor. He left the coat open, and wore one yellow glove and carried the other in the gloved hand. As he came out of the hotel he lit up the entire street. The scene was like a Maxfield Parrish painting until he turned the corner.

Kalakobé was supposed to work only during the daytime, but when we had banquets in the ballroom he was paid a little extra to come up and get the casseroles used in the banquet kitchen and, with a long iron hook, drag them into an elevator and down to his pantry. At first he came only during the serving of the meal, and left with the cooks, but then he found out that if he waited until the party was over and the tables were being cleared, the waiters would come back from the ballroom with a trayful of glasses in each hand, and in each of the glasses some drink would be left. After that he always stayed in the pantry and waited for the empty glasses. He poured all the drinks – champagne, Moselle, Burgundy, Bénédictine, rye, Scotch, Irish whiskey, brandy, and kümmel – into one pitcher, added lemon and sugar and ice, and bottled the whole mixture. What he did not drink himself, he took home and sold.

He came up to the ballroom during the daytime whenever he could get away from his casseroles, and particularly after large balls, when the place was filled with leftover scenery and flowers. While the carpenters and the cleaning-women came and went, he sat alone in a far corner of the room, in the dark, with a rose behind his ear, and only the glow of his cigarette giving away his presence. To protect himself against the cold draughts, he sometimes took one of the white felt covers that are used under table-cloths and wrapped it around himself like a robe. Then, with a bottle of his terrible drink on the floor beside him, with his feet spread, his arms loose and so placed that his two hands hung down over his knees, he sat there and made noises, sang quietly, hummed, or tapped with heel and toe, and watched himself in the many mirrors.

When Kalakobé wanted someone to talk to, he would come to see me in the assistant manager's office of the banquet department nearby. The first day he came, only his head came into the room. He expected to be ordered out, and when I let him remain he came in altogether, sat down on a silken *fauteuil*, and told me all about himself. He said that he was a Frenchman and that he wanted to be a doorman, that he was six and a half feet tall and would make a fine doorman, that he looked very well in uniform, and that perhaps I could fix it up so he could be a doorman at the Hotel Splendide. In the tailor's shop there was one unused doorman's uniform that fitted him exactly. Also a cap. Perhaps only as a night doorman to start with. He would learn English rapidly, immediately, he said. He could speak a little now – enough for a doorman.

I told Kalakobé that he would make a wonderful doorman, but all our doormen were Irish or English and, as far as I knew, all the doormen in the large and fine hotels in New York were either Irish or English. He said that this might be so, but that Goldfarb had a doorman who was not Irish or English. 'But Goldfarb is a florist,' I told him. He said that was all right, a florist, then – anything so he could be a doorman, any job where he could wear a uniform and advance himself in the world.

I inquired about jobs for him, and even sent him to one place which needed a doorman, but although he was acceptable, the uniform that went with the job was dirty, plain, and several sizes too small for Kalakobé, and he came back again.

This was about the season of the year when society moves to the South, and there was, as always, a lull in the business of fashionable hotels. Kalakobé had more time, and he came to see me very often. In the dim light of the reception room he would sit and talk to me. He spoke very slowly, and what he said was simple. His voice was soft, like a deep reed instrument. His thoughts crept around like rainworms, plain and with both ends the same – you could see where they were going and where they came from. His ideas were his own, free and private – it was not the usual tip-hungry conversation of hotel employees. He spoke of the city, of Africa, of trees, animals, an overcoat he wanted, or a Great Dane. His

French was exquisite and induced a pleasant drowsiness, like a sleeping tablet, and after a while the hypnosis worked and I was completely rested and asleep, but heard every word he said. He knew a wonderful story, which I asked him to tell over and over. I cannot reproduce his imitation of the voices of the animals as he spoke; but this was the story:

Long, long time ago, the Elephant was the King of the Animals; but the poor King was so old, so old that he no longer could attend to his duties or even think about them. He went about the whole day long with his mouth open, like a small child with the pain of its first teeth. A useless ruin of a King. The animals, however, went on acting as if they thought he left his mouth open because he was smiling, and all of them said: 'Oh, see what a good King we have, he is always smiling, he smiles without interruption!'

The dry season came, no rain fell, all the grasses were burnt by the sun. The Hare searches for fodder and finds none; no salad, no cabbages, nothing, absolutely nothing. But you know the Hare is filled with cunning and malice. When he sees the King's open mouth he jumps into it, and he crawls down into his stomach and gets busy eating the bowels. The Elephant feels nothing, his mouth stays open, he smiles without interruption. The Hare is a wicked animal. When he has eaten enough bowels, he goes up and gnaws the King's heart. Now the old King stops smiling, he closes his mouth, and he dies.

As soon as the Hare has eaten enough he wants to get out. Impossible; the door is closed. What is he to do? He returns to the stomach and sits down and thinks.

Outside the King, the animals in the meantime have discovered that he is dead. They are sad, they cry. The Ape goes to the young Elephant who will be his father's successor, and he says: 'Lord, to lessen our sorrow somewhat, permit that we bind the body of your father the King in scented grasses, lemon twigs, ferns, and palm leaves. What a terrible loss we have suffered!' And all the animals repeat in chorus: 'Yes, Lord, yes – let us protect his body so that it may stay as long as possible free of decay.'

The Ape then says to the other animals: 'Go search for herbs and grasses. I will keep with me the Rat, the Mouse, the Worm, and the Centipede, to empty the King's body.'

The Hare, who heard all this inside the King, wrapped himself quickly in what was left of the intestines, and the Ape had them taken out and thrown away far from the tree under which the King had died.

As soon as the Hare knew that all the animals had gone back, he crawled out and licked himself clean and then ran back to the King.

The Donkey and the Parrot came and held long speeches beside the grave. The Hare acted very sad. He threw himself down on the ground and lifted his eyes to heaven, and he cried: 'Woe – woe – woe unto us, how cruelly have we been stricken! And I was not here to close his eyes! My poor brothers, how will we bear it? We have lost the best of Kings. I was away on the island, visiting my wife's uncle – who also is near death – and when I came back I heard everyone say that the King, our good King, is dead. Let me weep! All of you share in this sorrow, my brothers; you all know what we have lost. But no one, no one but me, can know what a good heart, what an excellent heart, our King possessed.'

VI

A Night in Granada

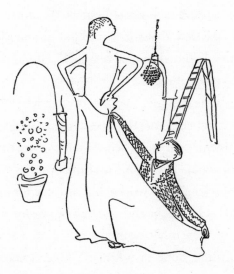

The annual Quat-z-Arts Ball was to be given at the Splendide that year. All the public rooms of the establishment had been engaged for this affair. It was to be known as 'A Night in Granada'. Weeks before it took place a large committee of patronesses arrived with two interior decorators, an orchestra leader, and a costume designer, and started to make plans for transforming the vast rooms into a replica of the city of Granada. Since Granada was at one time a Moorish city, I thought that both the party and Kalakobé would be benefited by having a black doorman in costume that night, and I suggested this to the energetic lady who was arranging the pageant and the *tableau vivant*. There were already close to a hundred people involved in one or the other, but when she saw Kalakobé, she took hold of my arm and said he must not be wasted out on the street. He was so handsome, she said, that she would put him in the centre of the festivities. In the triumphal march, Kalakobé should carry Isabella into the ballroom.

The costume designer and a couturier who was making the dress for Isabella came the next day and vaguely asked for Kalakobé. I sent them down below-stairs, where they saw him in the silver room. They came up full of praises, and the day after were back again to work out a costume for him. One of them looked at Kalakobé and said that he saw the whole thing in chartreuse. The other wanted a full-skirted effect, with a harem hem-line, done in postman's blue, a hooded silver-sequin burnoose over the shoulders. They disagreed, snatched swatches of material out of each other's hands, and became frigidly polite. Chartreuse won, and the costume designer knelt in front of Kalakobé and, with his mouth full of pins, draped him from the waist down in soft chartreuse flannel, while the chef phoned up for his casserolier and complained that the pots were mounting.

On the day of the party, while the decorations went up, Kalakobé was excused from his casseroles and appeared in the ballroom at about nine in the morning. The wide foyer of the Hotel Splendide had been transformed into Bib Rambla Square, and everywhere stood the pomegranate-trees that grow on the outskirts of Granada. The ballroom itself was the Plaza del Triunfo, and the balconies had been decorated to resemble Granada's most frequented promenade, the shady Alameda. Every window and door was now Moorish in architecture. The smaller rooms were lined with jasper and coloured marbles. In the ballroom a stage and a triumphal stairway had been built for the *tableau vivant*. In an antechamber that was to be used as a dressing-room the costumes for the pageant were being unpacked.

The main characters were Ferdinand and Isabella, Gonzalo de Córdoba, Diego Hurtado de Mendoza, Alonso Cano, Mohammed Ebn Al Ahmar, and Boabdil, and there were also many lesser figures out of the turbulent history of Granada. Isabella's gown was the most elaborate. It had been copied, rather freely, from a portrait of Ferdinand and Isabella by del Rincón, and was to be worn by Mme Julian Alexander Garrand. Mme Garrand, one of the hotel's best clients, was an elderly, asthmatic patroness of the Quat-z-Arts Ball who from year to year braced an uncertain social position by her appearance as the central figure of these spectacles. She had the breakable face of a porcelain puppet, that can risk neither to laugh nor to frown; the kind of face that one observes frequently in the shop windows of opticians, a lithograph reproduction of an oil portrait whereon it is evident that the artist has been instructed to stress refinement and culture. On these portraits one sees the kind of glasses that Mme Garrand wore, rimless, and attached to the end of a thin platinum chain, which hung across her left cheek. Without them, she was almost blind. She was distant and correct, and seemed nice until she spoke. The voice was a give-away. It came out between the baby lips a cold, ill wind, and to the trained ears of hotel employees it was the voice of a foe if anything went wrong.

For the supper that was to be served after the bacchanal, Mme Garrand had engaged a large table in the centre of the room. She tried her costume on several times. It was of golden brocade with a rhinestone brassière, out of which her old arms hung, heavy with bracelets. She was going to wear a diamond choker, and a large diamond diadem in her hair. A mantilla of old Spanish lace was tried and discarded; it hid her face.

Kalakobé was dressed at three in the afternoon. Except for a brief parade through the kitchens below, where he stopped all work, and a visit to the tailor, he never left the ballroom. In back of the scenery he had a bottle of his mixture, and from time to time he went there to refresh himself.

A pianist came about four and there was a short rehearsal. Kalakobé was placed in the centre of the *tableau vivant*, with Mme Garrand on his shoulder, and the pianist played Ravel's 'Pavane for a Dead Infanta'. After they had held the pose for a while, Kalakobé carried Mme Garrand down the stairs. He did it with much grace and without effort, for she was small and light. He was told to make a few turns, as if dancing, to put her down gently on the throne, and then lay himself at her feet. The music for this was L. von Meyer's 'Marche Marocaine', arranged by Berlioz. After all the participants in the pageant were seated in a circle, a troupe of hired Russian dancers was to dance a bolero. Then Raquel Meller would sing a few songs. After this, supper and dancing until three.

The energetic lady director screamed and pushed people into the formations she wanted, the two decorators argued about the lighting, several costumes were found to be missing, and a scenery man turned his ankle. Otherwise everything went very nicely. The florists folded their ladders and took them out; the coat-room girls came on duty, bringing their towels, soap, and check-stubs; the first musicians arrived and tuned their instruments; the ticket-takers slipped on their gloves; and the house detective picked his teeth and talked with the doorman. I went upstairs to change, and when I came down the orchestra was playing and the first guests were dancing.

At midnight the pageant began. The *tableau vivant* started off smoothly. Mme Julian Garrand was carried down the stairs as if she sat in the saddle of a prize stallion. Kalakobé made so festive an entrance with her that the thousand-and-some guests applauded. Mme Garrand, without glasses, smiled to the audience and bowed left and right. All the spotlights were on them. The sixty musicians fiddled and blew the last strains of the 'Marche Marocaine' and began the first bars of the bolero. The Russians came into the clear space in the centre of the ballroom, and Kalakobé, with Mme Julian Garrand on his shoulder, was in their midst. Perhaps he forgot, or perhaps the uncorked bottle and the loose music had worked on him. He refused to sit down or to put Mme Garrand on her throne. The Russians made faces at him as they danced and told him to set her down, and for the first time a number of the guests laughed. Most of them were too startled to do anything but watch as Kalakobé's body became rigid and a strange set of emotions took hold of him. He started a wild stamping, and went on dancing more and more wildly. The Russians left the floor to him. In desperation the orchestra followed his stamping and he conducted with his head, his legs, and arms. He obtained his best effects by throwing his partner into the air, as far as his and her outstretched arms would let their bodies part. Then he jerked her back again, passed her through his legs and up over his bent back, and decorations and jewellery fell out of her as out of a shaken Christmas tree. Once she got away from him and, with her mouth wide open, her beer-blonde hair streaming after her, fled towards the ring of people, but he caught her as one does a fleeing pullet and danced on. Up she flew and around and around, half mermaid, half witch, her legs bare, one shoe lost. The crowd roared at the end.

As we led Mme Garrand to the nearest elevator, Kalakobé was surrounded by admirers. He was soaking wet. His chartreuse flannel trousers were sticking to his limbs, his abdomen weaved in and out, and Raquel Meller sent someone for a drink and a towel. Mme Garrand didn't come down for supper.

The next morning Kalakobé sat alone in the ballroom. The kettle-drums were still there, looking a little like his copper pots downstairs. He sat on the north side of the Plaza del Triunfo, his feet away from him, his hands hanging over the knees. His eyes clung to each piece of scenery as it was carried out. While I was talking to him a bellboy came with a message from the manager.

'Gotdemn Cheeses Greisd! She's going to sue us for a million – the old pitch,' he said to the hotel's lawyer as I came in the door. 'Cheeses Greisd' was an exclamation which Mr Brauhaus used in every sentence when he was angry, alternating it with 'Gotdemn it'. Since there is continuous trouble in a hotel, he hardly ever spoke without using one or the other, and he was known by the employees as 'Jesus Christ'.

The lecture this time lasted an hour and three-quarters.

VII

The Hispano

The best source of information about the guests of the Hotel Splendide was not its credit department or the manager's office, but the couriers' dining-room. Under the heading of couriers came the chauffeurs, valets, butlers, nurses, and footmen who were not employed by the hotel but travelled with the guests as their personal servants. To them were assigned small rooms on the air-shafts; they were fed a *table d'hôte* menu in the couriers' dining-room. This apartment was a market for scandal, a place to which they all rushed and in which they lingered over the second and third cups of coffee, comparing notes, exchanging griefs and complaints. In English, French, German, Italian, and Spanish, and in all the various dialects of these languages, the infirmities and vices of the great were laid bare. The choicest filth was on tap in the couriers' dining-room, and from there it flowed out through the hotel; the best items travelled all the way up to the roof, where the Splendide's florist presided over his hothouse, and all the way down to the fourth basement, where the plumbers had their workshop.

One rainy April afternoon the telephone rang in my office. When I picked up the receiver, Pacifico, the valet of a Cuban marquis who was staying at the hotel, asked me whether I'd like to buy a car, a fine car, very cheap. If I wanted it, he said, would I buy it right away?

'This afternoon, please,' he urged. 'I will sell it at any price. I want to be rid of this car.'

The marquis's entourage occupied an entire floor. He was a small man, fat and smelling like a box of candy. He wore high heels, and his blue-black hair was glued to his head with pomade. Through the gossip of the couriers' dining-room, I had heard all about him. I knew that he was kind to Pacifico one day, embraced him, gave him watches and rings, sent him to the theatre, and beat him the next. I knew also that the marquis had a wife and many children in a palace in Havana,

that he had a house in Paris, that here in New York he resided
with a young girl he had brought along from France.

Her name was Nicole, but the Cuban's servants called her
La Platina because of her bleached yellow hair. She was a
routine French mannequin, nice enough, with a sweet face,
a small mouth and nose, and the glossy eyes of a Pomeranian.
On the street, smartly dressed in fine furs, her eyes shaded
by her hat, she was quite exciting. But in the corridors and
restaurants of the Splendide, where women of fortunate faces
and figures were as common as champagne bottles, no one
turned around to look at her.

The marquis never let her out of his sight. Half Indian,
dark as the fine cigars he smoked, he danced around her with
unending clumsy caresses. He held on to her, softly pushed her
before him, stroked her, sat her down, stood her up, and often
left one hand in her lap while he ate with the other. Pacifico
said that the marquis even undressed and bathed her himself.

The Platina was fond of tuberoses, but could not stand
their scent. The house florist had been instructed by the
marquis to fill her rooms with them and to cover them with
glass cloches.

The marquis had two cars. On cold days, when he wanted
to use the closed car, a Minerva, Pacifico telephoned the temperature of the marquis's apartment down to the doorman,
who then conveyed this information to the chauffeur. The
Minerva had a small thermometer on the instrument board.
When the marquis and the Platina got into the car an hour or

so later, they always found that it was the same temperature as their rooms.

The marquis's other car, an open Hispano, was painted *café au lait*, to match the Platina's two Afghan hounds, who always rode with her. The marquis hated dogs, but he put up with the hounds because the Platina loved them. The Hispano was long and low. Its tonneau was built by the Carrosserie Saoutchik. It had won the Prix d'Élégance at the Automobile Salon in Paris and later a race at Monaco. The seats were upholstered in leopard skin, and whenever the car was parked anywhere, it was hidden in a few moments by a throng of curious people.

The marquis was a devout Catholic, and every Sunday was driven in one car or the other to High Mass, and to confession on Saturdays. The object of his special devotion was the Madonna. On a chest just outside the marquis's bedroom stood an altar, and on it, in a small bed of Spanish lace, reposed an exquisitely dressed, much-blessed statue of the Virgin – antique and jewel-studded, with the Christ Child in her arms. There were other statues of the Virgin all over the apartment, and into the dashboard of the Hispano a miniature tabernacle had been built. There, behind glass in a tiny grotto, stood a silver statue of the Madonna, a few inches high. When the driver pushed a small button, the Madonna turned her back on the occupants of the car, so that she could not be offended by whatever went on in the deep, soft seats of the elegant vehicle.

On the day before Pacifico phoned and offered to sell me the Hispano, the Platina had been driving it in city traffic.

She had come up behind a truck loaded with steel girders that stuck far out in the rear. It was assumed in the couriers' dining-room that instead of putting her foot on the brake, the Platina had pushed down on the accelerator. Anyway, the car shot ahead, and the girders, smashing in on her, almost severed her head from her body. When the car was brought back to the hotel there were bloodstains on the leopard skin of the driver's seat. The wind-shield was broken; so were the headlights. The radiator was pushed against the engine.

The marquis wanted to kill himself. He had cursed the Madonna and then he had begun to weep. He had prayed on his knees all night. At daybreak he had instructed his servants to pack and had obtained passage on the next boat for France. Then he had told Pacifico to have the dogs destroyed and to get rid of the car. He never wanted to see the Hispano again.

The best firm of undertakers in New York City prepared the Platina for a voyage to Paris. They sent out for all the tuberoses that were to be had in New York, and a few hours after she was in their hands, with her eyes closed, Pacifico told his friends in the couriers' dining-room, she was prettier than she had ever been before.

All such things are not as important and terrible as they would be outside a large hotel. In a hotel too much is happening – the guests eat and drink, laugh and complain as at any time, the orchestras play in the restaurants, the hum of conversation is not a shade lower. Whatever is unpleasant is done quietly.

When someone has died in a hotel, two men carry a plain basket out of a side door early in the morning.

I did not want the Hispano. I knew that it was an expensive toy to keep, that it used too much gas, that replacements were costly. I did not like its colour or the leopard-skin upholstery. But Pacifico offered it to me for almost nothing – the repairs would cost more than the car – and so I bought it.

The next afternoon Kalakobé came to visit me in my office. I had been forgiven after the Quat-z-Arts episode, and Kalakobé had been kept on by the management; he was safely out of sight of the Garrands, among his casseroles. I told him about the Hispano. Immediately he wanted to see it, and so I took him over to the Splendide's garage and showed him the car. He turned the pink palms of his black hands towards it and said, '*Quelle merveille!*' At last he saw his chance for a job that required him to wear a uniform. Kalakobé said he would get one after the car was repaired and painted, and on his days off be my driver. In his free hours he would take care of the car and shine it – all out of love.

I could not get Kalakobé away from the Hispano until I agreed. He begged me to keep the leopard skin – just to have the bloodstains taken out. He straightened a rug and tried the emergency brake, which was on the outside of the tonneau. He went through the luggage compartment. He turned the Madonna around several times. In the glove compartment he found a tortoise-shell mirror and a cigarette case with emerald initials. He opened the cigarette case and discovered that inside there were rubies worked into the design of a tuberose. The case was worth more than the car.

During the next week Kalakobé spent a good deal of time in the chauffeurs' dressing-room of the Splendide's garage, and he stood outside the hotel and watched the guests' cars arrive. Every day he came to me with new ideas for uniforms. He made designs with crayons until he got one that he liked, and he was unhappy when I told him that it would not do. He had created a pale-blue Cossack coat with mustard piping, a bright collar, and gold buttons. I told him that nobody wore such uniforms, but he could not understand why, if he himself bought the outfit, he could not wear it. So I gave him a ticket to see *Othello* and told him to miss the first act and stand outside the Metropolitan, on the Thirty-ninth Street side, and watch the fine cars arrive. He came back from this performance and agreed in principle; but he said that one car had arrived with two chauffeurs, both wearing wide fur collars and fur hats. I explained to him that it was probably the car of some *parvenu*.

Finally he consented to a plain gun-metal gabardine coat and breeches, a black cap, black shoes, and puttees. The Splendide's uniform tailor made it for him at cost. Kalakobé looked very well in it.

On the day the Hispano was ready to run again, Kalakobé suggested that we go driving. With everything on him neat, his puttees shined, Kalakobé walked in front of me, now and then looking back to see if I was still following. At the car he smiled, stripped his lapis-lazuli ring and a gold ring from his fingers, and slipped his hands into tight black gloves. He walked once around the car, opened and closed the doors, and looked at the tyres. Then he polished the already gleaming wind-shield and the headlights, which which were as big as snare drums. Finally, without looking at me, he informed me that the most elegant way was for me to do the driving while he sat beside me. It was very chic, he said, for the boss to drive – he had seen it many times. Besides, he added, he didn't know how to drive.

So that was what we did. Whenever we took the car out, I drove and Kalakobé sat beside me. He opened and closed the doors, handed out fares on ferry-boats and tolls on bridges, paid for the gas, lit my cigarettes, and let people stare at him while he waited with the car. He called the car a convertible rooster, and told its pedigree to the crowds that gathered. His uniform was always pressed and spotless, his visor shined to its brightest possibilities.

VIII

The Homesick Bus Boy

In a corner of the main dining-room of the Splendide, behind an arrangement of screens and large palms that were bedded in antique Chinese vases, six ladies of uncertain age used to sit making out luncheon and dinner checks. When a guest at the Splendide called for the bill, it was brought to him in longhand – contrary to the practice in most other hotels in New York City – in purple ink, on fine paper decorated with the hotel crest. The six ladies, seated at a long desk near the exit to the kitchens, attended to that. And since there were periods when they had little to do, one of them, a Miss Tappin, found time to befriend the bus boy Fritzl, from Regensburg.

Fritzl was not much more than a child. He wore a white jacket and a long white apron, and he carried in his pocket a comb which he had brought all the way from Regensburg. A scene of the city was etched on the side of it. Fritzl's hair stood up straight, moist, and yellow, and he had the only red cheeks in the dining-room. When anyone spoke to him, his ears also turned red, and he looked as if he had just been slapped twice in the face.

Miss Tappin was very English. She had seen better days, and in her youth had travelled on the Continent. She detested the *maître d'hôtel*, the waiters, and the captains, but she was drawn to the lonesome bus boy, who seemed to be of nice family, had manners, and was shy. Fritzl did not like the *maître d'hôtel*, the waiters, or the captains either. Least of all he liked the waiter he worked for, a nervous wreck of a Frenchman who was constantly coming behind the screens and palms, saying 'Psst!' and dragging Fritzl out onto the floor of the restaurant to carry away some dirty dishes.

When Fritzl was thus called away, Miss Tappin would sigh and then look into the distance. She called Fritzl 'a dear', and said that he was the living image of a nephew of hers who was at Sandhurst – the son, by a previous marriage, of her late sister's husband, a Major Graves. 'What a pity!' Miss

Tappin would say whenever she thought of Fritzl. 'He's such a superior type, that boy. Such a dear. So unlike the bobtail, ragtag, and gutter-snipes around him. I do hope he'll come through all right!' Then she would sigh again and go back to her bills. Every time Fritzl passed the long desk, whether with butter, water-bottles, or dirty dishes, a quick signal of sympathy passed between them.

The conversations with Fritzl afforded Miss Tappin an exquisite weapon with which to irritate the other five ladies who shared the desk – women who came from places like Perth Amboy, Pittsburgh, and Newark. With Fritzl leaning on her blotter, she could discuss such topics as the quaintness of Munich and its inhabitants and the charm and grandeur of the Bavarian Alps. These beautiful mountains neither Fritzl nor Miss Tappin had ever seen. Regensburg is not far away from the Alps, but Fritzl's parents were much too poor ever to have sent him there. Miss Tappin's stay in Munich had been limited to a half-hour wait between trains at the railroad station while she was on her way to visit her sister in Budapest.

Regensburg, however, she soon came to know thoroughly from Fritzl, who often spread a deck of pocket-worn postcards and calendar pictures on the desk in front of her. These views showed every worthwhile street corner and square of his beloved city. He acquainted her with Regensburg's history and described its people and the surrounding country. He read her all the letters he received from home, and gradually Miss Tappin came to know everybody in Regensburg.

'Dear boy,' she would say, touching his arm, 'I can see it all clearly. I can picture your dear mother sitting in front of her little house on the banks of the Danube – the little radish garden, the dog, the cathedral, and the wonderful stone bridge. What a lovely place it must be!'

Then her eyes would cloud, for Miss Tappin had the peculiar British addiction to scenes that are material for postcards. Into the middle of these flights always came the nervous 'Psst!' of the old French waiter. Then Fritzl would lift his apron, stow the postcards away in the back pocket of his trousers, and run. When he passed that way later with a tray of dirty dishes, he sent her his smile, and again when he came back with an armful of water-bottles or a basin of cracked ice and a basket of bread. They recognised each other as two nice people do, walking their dogs in the same street.

Fritzl's service table stood in another corner of the restaurant, and near it was another palm in another Chinese vase. When he was not at Miss Tappin's desk or in the kitchen or busy with his dirty dishes, Fritzl hid behind this palm. He was afraid of everyone, even the guests. He came out from behind his palm only when his waiter called him, or when the orchestra played Wagner, Weber, or Strauss music, or when I, his other friend in the hotel, passed by.

By this time I was assistant manager in the banquet department, but Fritzl was not afraid of me. I was his friend because I, too, came from Regensburg. Sometimes when I appeared in the restaurant, Fritzl would lean out from behind his palm and say in a hoarse whisper, '*Du*, Ludwig, have you a minute for me?' Once he put his arm around my neck and started to walk with me through the dining-room as if we were boys in Regensburg. When I told him that that was not done, he looked hurt, but later, in the pantry, he forgave me and told me all the latest and most important news of Regensburg.

Another time he showed me a little book he had made out of discarded menus. In this book he had written down what he earned and what he spent. His income was eight dollars a week, and his expenses, including an English lesson at one dollar, were seven. In three years, he calculated, he would have enough money to go back to Regensburg. I told him he could make much more money if he attended to his job and got to be a waiter, and he said he would try. But Fritzl was very bad dining-room material. He was slow, earnest, and awkward. A good waiter jumps, turns fast, and has his eyes everywhere. One can almost tell by watching a new man walk across the room whether he will be a good or an indifferent waiter. One can also tell, as a rule, if he will last.

We sometimes took a walk together, Fritzl and I, usually up or down Fifth Avenue, in the lull between luncheon and dinner. One day, in the upper window of a store building near Thirty-fourth Street, Fritzl saw an advertisement that showed a round face smoking a cigar. Under the face was written, 'E. Regensburg & Sons, Havana Cigars'. From that day on, Fritzl always wanted to walk downtown towards

Thirty-fourth Street. He would point up at the window as we passed and say, 'Look, Ludwig – Regensburg.'

He also liked to stop in front of St Patrick's Cathedral, because it reminded him of the Dom in Regensburg. But St Patrick's was not half as big as the Dom, he said, and its outside looked as if it were made of fresh cement, and its bells were those of a village church. He was very disappointed by the interior as well.

Once I took him on an excursion boat up the Hudson. 'Fritzl, look,' I said to him, 'isn't this river more beautiful than the Danube?'

He was quiet for several miles. Opposite Tarrytown, he said, 'It's without castles. I have not seen a single castle, only smokestacks.' Up at Poughkeepsie, he pointed to the railroad bridge and said, 'Look at it, and think of the stone bridge across the Danube at Regensburg. And besides, where is Vienna on this river, or a city like Budapest?' For the rest, he said, it was all right.

I sometimes wondered why Fritzl should love Regensburg, for I knew that he had grown up there in misery. His parents lived on the outskirts of the city and worked as tenants on a few soggy acres planted with radishes and cabbages. The land lay along the river and was submerged whenever the water rose. The Danube rose very often. The place where they lived was called Reinhausen. One came to it by crossing an old stone bridge and walking through another city, which was to Regensburg what Brooklyn is to New York. The people who lived in this small Brooklyn always explained why they were living there – the air was better, the view nicer, it was better for their children, quieter – but they all excused themselves. The place resembled Brooklyn also in that one got lost there very easily and that no cab-driver in Regensburg could find his way there without asking a policeman for directions.

When I asked Fritzl why he loved Regensburg so much, his answer sounded like Heinrich Heine. 'Do you remember the seven stone steps,' he said, 'the worn stones that lead down from the Street of St Pancraz to the small fish market? The old ivy-covered fountain whose water comes from the mouth of two green dolphins? The row of tall oaks with a bench between every other pair of trees? The sand-pit next to the fountain where children play, where young girls walk arm in arm, where the lamp-lighter arrives at seven, and where, sitting on a bench, I can see, between the leaning walls of two houses, a wide strip of moving water – the Danube – and beyond it my parents' house? There I grew up. There every stone is known to me. I know the sound of every bell, the name of every child, and everyone greets me.'

Like a child himself then, he would repeat over and over, 'Oh, let me go home. I want to go home to Regensburg. Oh, I don't like it here. What am I here? Nobody. When I told Herr Professor Hellsang I wanted to come to America, he said to me, "*Ja*, go to America, become a waiter – the formula for every good-for-nothing. But remember, America is the land where the flowers have no perfume, where the birds lack song, and where the women offer no love." And Herr Professor Hellsang was right. It is so. Oh, I want to go back to Regensburg!'

When we returned to the hotel from an afternoon walk, Fritzl always disappeared into the Splendide's basement, where the dressing-rooms for the bus boys were, and changed his clothes. The other bus boys' lockers were lined with clippings from *La Vie Parisienne* and with pictures of cyclists and boxers. The door of Fritzl's was covered with views of Regensburg.

One evening Fritzl came up from his locker to assist at a dinner-party given by Lord Rosslare, who had ordered a fairly good dinner, long and difficult to serve. He was a moody client, gay one day, unbearable the next. When he complained, his voice could be heard out on the street. Rosslare's table was in the centre of the room, and next to it was a smaller table on which to ladle out the soup, divide the fish into portions, and carve the rack of lamb. The *maître d'hôtel* and his assistant supervised all this. Fritzl's waiter was moist with nervousness and fear. Everything went well, however, until the rack of lamb was to be carved.

The lamb had arrived from the kitchen and stood on an electric heater on Fritzl's service table behind the palm. Next to Lord Rosslare stood the *maître d'hôtel*, who intended to carve. He had the knife in one hand and a large fork in the other. He looked along the edge of the knife and tested its sharpness. The old waiter polished the hot plates in which the lamb was to be served and then carried the stack of them and the sauce to the table. Because the *maître d'hôtel* was shouting at him to hurry up, he told Fritzl to follow with the rack of lamb. All Fritzl had to do was to take the copper casserole and follow him. To save time, they walked across the dance-floor instead of around it. Rosslare leaned back and complained about the slowness of the service. The *maître d'hôtel* stamped his feet and waved the carving-knife. With his mouth stretched, he signalled to the old waiter and Fritzl so they could read his lips: '*Dépêchez-vous, espèces de salauds*.'

All this made Fritzl nervous, and in the middle of the dance-floor he tripped and fell. The rack of lamb jumped out of the casserole. Then an even more terrible thing happened. Fritzl, on all fours, crept over to the lamb, picked it up calmly and put it back in the casserole, licked his slippery fingers, got to his feet, and, to everyone's horror, carried it over to the table to be served.

Rosslare laughed. The whole dining-room laughed. Only Monsieur Victor, the *maître d'hôtel*, was not amused. He retired to his office and bit into his fist. Next day the captain at that station got a severe reprimand. The old waiter was to be laid off for two weeks and Fritzl was to be discharged.

In a hotel that employed hundreds of people there were always changes in personnel. And fortunately an old Greek who had been attendant in the men's washroom in the banquet department left on that day for his homeland. His job was vacant, and Fritzl got it.

In the washroom, Fritzl was his own master. There were no *maîtres d'hôtel*, captains, and waiters to be afraid of. No one said 'Psst!' and 'Come here!' to him. He began to be more cheerful. One of his uncles, he told me, a veteran of the War of 1870, had, in recognition of his services, been given the washroom concession at the Walhalla, a national shrine built of marble, like the washroom in the banquet department of the Splendide, and situated not far from Regensburg.

Every morning Fritzl went down to the storeroom and got his supply of brushes, soap, ammonia, and disinfectants. Next he went to the linen-room and exchanged his dirty towels for clean ones. Then he put his washroom in order. He whistled while he polished the knobs and handles and water-faucets, and when everything was shining he conscientiously flushed all the toilets and pressed the golden buttons that released a spray of water into the porcelain basins, to see that they were working. If any of the plumbing was out of order, he telephoned down to the engineers. At noon he reported to the banquet office and was told whether any parties would take place during the afternoon or evening. If the banquet-rooms were not engaged, he was free the rest of the day.

When Fritzl worked, he made good money. He soon learned to brush the guests off and to hold them up at the narrow door so that none escaped without producing a dime or a quarter. In busy seasons he sometimes made as much as thirty dollars a week.

He became more tolerant of America and found that, contrary to the belief of Herr Professor Hellsang, birds do sing here and flowers do have a perfume. Late at night, after he had locked up the men's room, Fritzl arranged his coins in neat stacks and entered the total in his book. He often came into the banquet office, when everyone else was gone, and asked to use my typewriter. On this machine, using two fingers, he slowly composed glowing prospectuses of the hotel – letters that his mother would proudly show around. On the hotel's stationery he wrote that the Splendide was the most luxurious hotel in the world; that it was twenty-two stories high; that it had seven hundred apartments, any one of which was better furnished than the rooms in the castle of the Duke of Thurn und Taxis in Regensburg; that in these apartments lived the richest people in America; that he was employed at a lucrative income in the Department of Sanitation; and that he would probably come home for a short visit in the summer.

IX

The New Suit

Fritzl did not go to Europe the next summer; he worked one more year at the hotel, and what the banks say in their advertisements is true. When you save your money and regularly deposit small amounts, you find yourself in possession of a respectable sum. With frugal living, with an occasional tip on the market, Fritzl found himself the owner of three thousand five hundred dollars.

At the end of the season, in June, when the last wedding was over and the ballroom cleared for painting and repairs, he said that he had succeeded in finding a ship on which he could work his way over, and that he would meet me in London. He wanted to go to London to have the suit made in which he would arrive in Regensburg.

The problem of outfitting himself for his homecoming had been with him constantly for months. The suit was the only good suit he ever wanted. After that he did not care what he wore, he said. He said that he wanted to arrive in Regensburg 'looking like a gentleman'.

In pursuit of this project he had combed advertisements in the papers, looked into all the clothing-store windows; he had also spent hours leaning over Miss Tappin's desk. Miss Tappin had tried to discourage pinchback suits and pinstriped double-breasted flannels. She had stopped once in front of Brooks Brothers' and almost agreed that what was in the window was right and good, but then she had begun to reminisce about British tailors and told Fritzl what a pity it was that he could not have a suit made in London, at a shop such as that where her father and her brother-in-law traded; at John's and Pegg's in Clifford Street, or at Anderson and Sheppard's. The suit would be about a hundred dollars, but it would be right.

Fritzl, though he counted every penny, did not seem to mind that expense. When I told him I would not go to London just to get him a suit, that he could get one which would still be a sensation in Regensburg for half that money here in New York, he moped down in his washroom, but finally he went with Miss Tappin and they ended up once more at Brooks Brothers', buying two suits: one – against Miss Tappin's advice – a light grey flannel, double-breasted, with white stripes; the other conservative and dark grey. After the tailor had made the alterations, Fritzl came back and walked up and down in front of all the ballroom mirrors and looked at himself from every angle.

He sat with the new suit in the banquet office and pictured his arrival in Regensburg – his mother's and his father's pride, and how mad everybody else would be. That part gave him the most pleasure. He took hold of the sleeve of my coat and said, 'Ludwig, can you imagine Professor Hellsang? Can you picture him? Can you see his face when he sees me in this suit? Maybe he will be at the railroad station. Sunday afternoons he always eats out in the restaurant of the depot and then walks up and down watching the trains arrive. I hope he'll be there—'

His joy was trebled when I told him that we would not arrive at the railroad station, because I was taking the car.

'Ah,' he said, 'they'll be twice as mad. We'll pass the Professor in the street, most probably, several times a day.'

He packed the suit away carefully, and did not wear it again until we were in Europe. He wore the dark one. The light grey he wanted for his entrance into Regensburg.

'I don't think a Hispano-Suiza has ever been seen in Regensburg,' he said on the road from Nancy to Strasbourg.

And later on he said, 'The Duke of Thurn und Taxis has only a Mercedes. Perhaps in Munich there might have been one, but I hardly think so.'

Fritzl's hopes were fully realised when something happened to the car. It had got stuck several times, but never in a better place than on the Sunday morning when we drove into Regensburg. It stopped, being out of gas, precisely in front of the main portal of the cathedral, just as High Mass came to an end.

It was a bright morning. The post office which stands directly opposite the cathedral was newly painted. Between the high crosses on top of the spires the sun shone down on the long, low car, and out of the cathedral came the last strains of the High Mass. Down the stone steps poured the Regensburgers. They were, by a benevolent arrangement of lamp-posts, buildings, statuary, and a barricade around a torn-up portion of the square, forced to thin out and pass the car in line, to the left and right.

The children pointed at the Hispano, soldiers and servant girls walked slowly by. The *beau monde* tried to pass quickly – and only when they were at a safe distance did they turn to look in such a fashion that their field of vision included the church, the lamp-posts, and part of the post office, so that one could not say that they were staring at the Hispano.

The uppermost class – the Burgomaster, the Rector of the Lycée at which we had studied, and their friends and relatives – did not even look that much. They betook themselves to the windows of a corsetière and a bookshop, and studied the scene in the reflection of the glass with their backs towards the cathedral and the car.

When most of them had gone, I drove Fritzl across the stone bridge to Reinhausen and I went back to the brewery that belonged to my grandfather and waited for Fritzl to come back to join me.

I stopped for a while in the long entrance hall of the brewery – a tunnel that went through the main building and opened out into a garden filled with old chestnut-trees, iron tables and chairs, a bandstand, and stacks of barrels.

All this was as familiar to Fritzl as it was to me. Fritzl, when he was a little boy, came all the way to the brewery every evening, barefooted, and solemnly carrying a beer-jug in front of him; a stone jug that broke if it ever was dropped. He came for beer for his father, not the regular beer, but a beer that cost only three pfennigs a quart.

This beer should really have been thrown away, but many people would not have had anything to drink at all then, and the brewers of Regensburg set the low price of three pfennigs a quart, so that it did not become a begging matter, and the poor could drink a lot. Its alcoholic content was as high as that of good beer.

The place where beer was served was a vaulted hall between the tunnel and the restaurant. It was badly lit day and night, its stone floor always wet. This room had an entrance from the restaurant and another from the tunnel.

Against one wall a wooden platform of heavy rafters was built. It inclined somewhat, and on it stood the beer barrels. Every time a barrel was tapped some beer was spilled and flowed down into a basin that stood on the floor. More beer was spilled when the brewboy who served it filled the glasses. This spilled beer was caught in a brass sink and also flowed down to the basin. The waste beer caught in that basin was called 'Convent' beer on account of the poverty of the nuns.

The good beer was passed to the waitresses across a counter. This counter was covered with a sheet of hammered pewter, and it had always looked to me, as a child, like a drawing of the sunrise. In the centre was the sun, a funnel-shaped opening. From this, small gutters like sunbeams reached to all the corners of the counter. All around, where the rays stopped, brewers' symbols and tools were stencilled into the metal. Over the sun was my grandfather's name: Ludwig Fischer; under it the Bavarian coat of arms, and across the outer edge the legend: 'Hopfen und Malz, Gott erhalts'. Two beer barrels, on the left and right sides of the lower edge, completed the design, and the right-hand barrel had the date of the founding of the brewery.

When the mugs of beer were placed on this counter the foam was brushed off them and it ran down the side of the steins, liquefied, and collected in the gutters running down to the centre and into the funnel. A pipe drained this also into the basin which stood under the barrels.

At about five, the children waited outside in the tunnel. At that time hundreds of beers were served, and the Convent beer became a little more alive than during the quiet hours. The children handed their mugs through a side window, the brewboy dipped them into the basin of Convent beer, and out of the goodness of his heart, and because a brewer needs good will among the poor, he put a good shot of real beer on top of the stale soup and handed it back. With most serious faces the children streamed out into the night. The little bare feet of boys and girls went like machines under them because their fathers were connoisseurs of this mean brew. They could detect time lost looking into a shop window. When they got home too late with it a thrashing awaited them.

I remembered all this as I sat in the restaurant, and thought how things stand still here – the same smell, the same pot of Convent beer, the same noises and the same faces all about me.

After a while Fritzl came and sat down with me and ordered a beer. When he had got used to the light, he nudged me and pointed to a table a few feet away and said, 'Look! There he is – it's Hellsang.'

I looked and recognised Professor Hellsang. We nodded, and he nodded sharply. Fritzl and I had been in his class, and his appearance brought back more memories of the unhappiness of German youth.

Fritzl had been recommended by the priest of his parish as a smart and good boy, and the city fathers had made it possible for him, along with a dozen other poor boys, to attend the Lycée. But they should also have fed and dressed him.

Fritzl had always been hungry. He had had to wear his brothers' suits after they had outgrown them; he was the smallest of the four. His little pants had stood up almost by themselves; they shone like antique tiles that once had been green. There were patches on the knees and on the seat, patches on the elbows of the coat. These terrible little suits exhaled years of little boys' untidinesses; the spilled beer, unmade beds, and the closeness of low rooms.

We had sat together on the same bench in the Regensburg Lycée. I did not mind Fritzl. He was my friend, and I was used to the smell. But Professor Hellsang used to object to Fritzl and to his suit. He called him 'Cabbage Soup'. He stopped at his place as he paraded up and down between the rows of pupils, sniffed the air, asked a boy to open a window, and said: 'The eternal cabbage soup!' He looked down at Fritzl and advised him that when he ran home with his father's beer he might try falling near the Artillery Armoury, where the stables are; it would be a holiday for him, a change for once from the smell of eternal cabbage cooking.

Such suggestions were routine to us, they no longer hurt. But once Hellsang stopped and carefully started to examine Fritzl. He looked at him very closely, went over him inch by inch; the boy's hair was brushed, his ears were clean, his neck washed, scrubbed. Then he examined Fritzl's clothes. Finally he found something. The sleeves were like the edges of an old carpet, all tassels and stuck-together fringe.

The Professor picked Fritzl up and stood him on the bench

so that he faced the class of well-dressed boys, and then he reached into several pockets until he found a pair of scissors. With these he carefully trimmed the ends of the sleeves and brushed the cut threads into his hand; he burned them in the oven, and then very deliberately went to the washstand, pushed back his sleeves, took off his cuffs, and made a careful and long job of washing his hands.

While he dried them, he came back and with mock solicitude patted Fritzl on the head and said that it was a pity about the cabbage soup; that he would be glad to have the suit cleaned for Fritzl, if only he had another to wear in the meantime. 'A few more patches and then we'd be almost elegant, eh, Fritzl?' He addressed the class then and asked them whether one of the boys could not ask his parents for an old suit for Fritzl.

In the courtyard of that school a door led into a woodshed where we sometimes played and hid during recess. There I found Fritzl.

He was sitting in a corner weeping. It seemed as if some invisible person continually kicked him. His face was hot and dirty, smeared with tears. He looked up and tried to form words with his shapeless mouth, and between sobs he said: 'I'll pay him back – oh, I'll pay him back for this. Oh, wait till I grow up, I'll pay him back.' Then he turned his face away, bit his hand, and began kicking the ground with his legs.

This happened not so many years ago – and here across the room sat the Herr Professor. He hadn't changed much since those terrible days.

Fritzl got up and walked over to the Professor's table, clicked his heels, and bent low. The Professor put down his paper, greeted him, and asked him to sit down. I wondered what would happen. There was some conversation, and for a while I was fearful, but both smiled, and presently Fritzl bowed and got up again. He came back to get me, and as we sat down with the Herr Professor, Fritzl said that he had wanted to invite the Herr Professor for dinner at the Hotel Maximilian, but that the Herr Professor had a meeting at the Ministry of Culture in Munich the next day and could not come.

The best restaurant in Regensburg, one that a Professor never could afford, is the restaurant of the Hotel Maximilian; but there are much better ones in Munich, said Fritzl, and so we ended up by offering to drive the Herr Professor to Munich – and to have dinner with him there.

We returned to our table.

'Just wait,' said Fritzl. 'Just let me alone. I've got it all planned. I'll pay him back. I have a little speech to make – and he'll have to listen to it.'

We were a little late starting the next morning. It was always hard to get Fritzl out of bed. When we were ready and had had our breakfast, the problem of getting money came up. Professor Hellsang was sitting downstairs in the lobby of the Maximilian, with a small bag, waiting. The head waiter of the hotel said we might get a cheque cashed at the Dresdner Bank, but on account of the inflation it was hard to get any large amount, or rather any amount we might ask for would be too bulky to manage. 'Large' meant one or two billion marks. He said we might get it because we had American Traveller's Cheques. I went to the bank and tried to get a hundred-dollar cheque cashed. The Dresdner Bank called up several other banks and finally, with the aid of someone who wanted foreign exchange, we got it. I had to call Fritzl to bring a travelling-bag to put in the packages of money. Two employees at the bank were busy counting the bundles and packing it away.

The Professor stood and watched. Some were old fifty-mark bills, and on each bill '500 MARKS' had been printed across the old amount. Other bills were for a thousand, and one package was made up of ten-thousand-mark bills. There were some left over, and we put them into the glove compartment of the Hispano. And then we got in, the Professor seated between us, and we raced all the way to Munich.

No one said a word. I knew that Fritzl was rehearsing his speech – he sat silent, his lips compressed, and looked straight ahead. We dropped the Herr Professor at the Ministry of Culture and arranged to meet him there again later, and then we went out to Nymphenburg.

Fritzl still seemed preoccupied. When I looked at him and said, 'Well, what are you going to say to him?' he smiled and said, 'Just wait – you'll see.'

The Royal Palace in Nymphenburg was deserted. We drove back into Munich, past the railroad station to the Ministry, and waited. The Professor came, and Fritzl helped him into the car, addressing him by his title, with great ceremony, as always.

We drove off to a small, distinguished, hidden restaurant that stands on the Platzl right next to the Hofbräuhaus.

This restaurant has two public rooms, one for the well-to-do middle class, the other for the rich. Built into both rooms is a square, ample oven made of grass-green tiles. Both rooms are panelled in almost black stained oak. Nibelungen scenery fills the space between panelling and ceiling in the lesser room.

The room into which we went, the one on the right, offers antlers, a portrait by Kaulbach, and over the door a nude with her backside turned to the room. The door under this picture opens out into a dimly lit passage with a stone floor. When it is open, the scent of stale beer, latrines, and carriage horses comes into the room. This aroma, the smoke of expensive cigars, and fresh bread, identify the excellent South German restaurant.

The car outside was surrounded by people. Fritzl brought the Gladstone bag filled with money into the room. The proprietor advanced with two deep bows to every step he took. He pushed his help around, hissed at the waiters, and three chairs were pulled by three of them. Three menus, each one as wide as an American newspaper, were put in our hands. Everything on them was crossed out and all the prices covered with stickers. Only in the centre of the printed card was a vacant column with lines left for handwritten special dishes. This was half filled; the *plats du jour* and their prices were there.

The Piccolo swished flies off the tables with his napkin. Professor Hellsang, very short-sighted now, held the card close to his nose, and in the fearful and ancient gesture with which he corrected our lessons, his finger wandered down the list on the side where the prices were.

Herring fillet in wine sauce, eight hundred thousand marks.
Home-made Sulze, five hundred thousand marks.
Noodle soup, three hundred thousand marks.
Kraftsuppe mit Ei, four hundred thousand marks.
Ragout mit Spätzle, one million marks.
Paprika-Schnitzel mit Reis, one million five hundred thousand marks.

'I don't know what to choose,' said the Professor.

Fritzl announced to the Professor and me that we were his guests. He put the big menus away and called the proprietor and explained to him that we wanted a good dinner. We wanted some caviar, some *Truites au bleu*, and a *Poularde rôtie*, with some compote.

'Ah, yes, but certainly,' said the proprietor, 'but the price, *mein Herr?*'

'The price,' Fritzl explained to him, 'usually appears on the bill at the end of the meal.'

'After the *Poularde*,' Fritzl continued, 'we want some asparagus with *Hollandaise*.'

Now the proprietor clasped his hands together hard, and let them remain in the position of prayer. Asparagus, he said, a thousand apologies, asparagus he had not, he could not afford to keep it.

Fritzl complained about the kind of restaurant he was running. The man looked stupid, hopeless, and embarrassed, and I told him he could send someone to Dallmeyer's, Munich's de luxe delicatessen store which is located close to the Feldherrnhalle, and ask for the best they had; large, fat, white Belgian asparagus – enough for three people.

The proprietor almost kicked the Piccolo through the door, to hurry him to Dallmeyer's shop. In the meantime we ate the caviar, very small portions of it.

Professor Hellsang sat between us, silent and uncomfortable. He looked into the wine-glasses as they were filled, and then he moistened the tip of a finger and with it picked up breadcrumbs that lay about his butter-plate. He wolfed his food down and nibbled clean every bone of the *Poularde*, holding a leg in his hands. When the asparagus came, we each had six stalks, nice and white and large, with excellent *Hollandaise* of just the right consistency. The Herr Professor ate one, then one more, and after a while a third.

Suddenly he paused and looked around. Fritzl looked at me. Now, I thought, the time is ripe. Fritzl leaned across the table and said, 'Herr Professor –' He repeated, 'Oh – Herr Professor,' and reached to touch him. But Professor Hellsang did not hear him.

The Herr Professor tried to catch the eye of a waiter; then he asked to be excused. He walked to the kitchen entrance, and as he took two steps up to the service door, I saw that the Herr Professor had holes in his socks, and a disorderly pair of trousers with frayed cuffs. Fritzl looked after him and said to me, 'My God, this cannot be – look at Professor Hellsang, a German professor, with holes in his socks and torn trousers.'

The Professor had disappeared into the kitchen. Presently he returned with a piece of wrapping paper. He sat down at the table, and his eyes were on his three remaining asparagus stalks. He took them one after another, and carefully wrapped them up in the paper he had brought. Then he tucked them away inside his coat.

At last he said, talking down to the table, without raising his eyes, in a toneless voice and with much clearing of his throat, 'This asparagus is for my wife.' … He said, too, that neither Frau Professor Hellsang nor he had had asparagus since before the war, or, for that matter, coffee or tea … that this little gift would make his return from Munich a double joy … that she would be so grateful to us for having made it possible.

We ordered coffee and cigars. Out of his waistcoat pocket the Professor produced a pair of scissors and offered to clip the ends of our cigars. He smoked his own very slowly, and we sat and waited until it was time for his train to Regensburg.

X

The Ballet Visits the Magician

The management of the banquet department kept on file the addresses of a number of men who were magicians, fortune-tellers, or experts with cards. One of these entertainers frequently appeared at the end of the small dinner-parties which were given in the private suites of the Splendide in those days. Our entertainers had acclimatised their acts to the elegance of the hotel, and the magicians, for example, instead of conjuring a simple white rabbit from their hats, cooked therein a soufflé Alaska or brought out a prize puppy with a rhinestone collar. When young girls were present, the magician pulled from their noses and out of corsages Cartier clips, bracelets, and brooches, which were presented to them with the compliments of the host.

Among the best and most talented of our performers was Professor Maurice Gorylescu, a magician who did some palmistry on the side. He came to the hotel as often as two or three times a week. After coffee had been served, he entered the private dining-room, got people to write any number they wanted to on small bits of paper, and held the paper to their foreheads. Then he guessed the numbers they had written down and added them up. The total corresponded to a sum he found on a dollar bill in the host's pocket. He did tricks with cards and coins, and he told people about the characteristics and the habits of dress and speech of friends long dead. He even delivered messages from them to the living.

At the end of his séances he went into some vacant room nearby, sank into a chair, and sat for a while with his hand over his eyes. He always looked very tired. After about half an hour he shook himself, drank a glass of water slowly, then ate something, and went home.

Professor Gorylescu earned a good deal of money. His fee for a single performance was a flat hundred dollars, and he sometimes received that much again as a tip from a grateful host. But although he worked all during the season, he spent everything he made, and often asked for and received his fee in advance. All he earned went to women – to the support of a Rumanian wife in Bucharest, to an American one who lived somewhere in New Jersey, and to what must have been a considerable number of New York girls of all nationalities to whom he sent little gifts and flowers.

When he came to the hotel during the day, he would hang his cane on the door-knob outside the ballroom office, ask me for a cigarette, and after a while steal a look at the book in which the reservations for small dinners were recorded. Very casually, and while talking of other things, he would turn the leaves and say something like 'Looks very nice for the next two months', and put the book back. It took only a few seconds, but in this time his trick mind had stored away all the names, addresses, dates, and telephone numbers in the book. He went home with this information, called up the prospective party-givers, and offered his services.

There was a strict rule that no one should be permitted to look at these reservations, certainly not Professor Gorylescu, but I liked him, and when I was on duty in the ballroom office I pretended not to see him when he peeked in the book. I also gave him leftover *petits fours*, candies, and after-dinner mints, of which he was very fond. He waved good-bye with his immense hands, asked me to visit him soon at his home, and suggested that I bring along some *marrons glacés*, pastry, nuts – anything like that – and then he left, a stooping, uncouth figure bigger than our tallest doorman.

Maurice Gorylescu lived on one of the mediocre streets that run between Riverside Drive and West End Avenue. He had a room in one of the small marble mansions that are common in that neighbourhood. The rooming-house in which Gorylescu lived was outstanding even among the ornate buildings of that district. It was a sort of junior Frankenstein castle, bedecked with small turrets, loggias, and balconies. It faced the sidewalk across a kind of moat – an air-shaft for the basement windows – traversed by a granite bridge. The door was hung on heavy iron hinges that reached all the way across.

In character with this house was the woman who rented its rooms, a Mrs Houlberg. She stood guard much of the time at the window next to the moat, looking out over a sign that read 'Vacancies'. She always covered three-quarters of her face with her right hand, a long hand that lay diagonally across her face, the palm over her mouth, the nails of the fingers stopping just under the right eye. It looked like a mask, or as if she always had a toothache.

Gorylescu lived on the top-floor front and answered to four short rings and one long one of a shrill bell that was in Mrs Houlberg's entrance hall. Badly worn banisters led up four flights of stairs. From the balcony of his room one could see the time flash on and off in Jersey and the searchlights of a battleship in the Hudson. The room was large, and newly painted in a wet, loud red, the colour of the inside of a water-melon. A spotty chartreuse velvet coverlet decorated a studio couch. Facing this was a chair, a piece of furniture such as you see in hotel lobbies or club cars, covered with striped muslin and padded with down. There was also a Sheraton highboy, which stood near a door that led into an adjoining room which was not his. From the ceiling hung a cheap bazaar lamp with carmine glass panes behind filigree panels. On shelves and on a table were the photographs of many women; in a box, tied together with ribbons in various colours, he kept packets of letters, and in a particular drawer of the highboy was a woman's garter, an old girdle, and various other obvious and disorderly trophies.

Gorylescu reclined on the studio bed most of the time when he was at home. He wore a Russian blouse that buttoned under the left ear, and he smoked through a cigarette-holder a foot long. One of his eyes was smaller and lower down in his face than the other, and between them rose a *retroussé* nose, a trumpet of a nose, with cavernous nostrils. Frequently and with great ceremony he sounded it into an immense handkerchief. His cigar-coloured skin was spotted as if with a bluish kind of buckshot, and when he was happy he hummed through his nose, mostly the melody of a song whose title was 'Tu sais si bien m'aimer'.

At home he was almost constantly in the company of women. He made the acquaintance of some of them at parties where he had entertained. They brought him gifts, and if they were fat and old, he read their minds and told them things of the past and future. At other times he went looking for girls along Riverside Drive, humming through his nose, and dragging after him a heavy cane whose handle was hooked into his coat pocket.

He went to various other places to find girls. He picked them up at dance-halls in Harlem, on the subway, on roller coasters. He easily became acquainted with them anywhere, and they came to his room willingly and took their chances with him. I always thought I might find one of them, dead and naked, behind the Japanese screen, where he kept a rowing-machine on which he built himself up. For the space of time that I knew him, love, murder, and this man seemed to be close together and that room the inevitable theatre for it.

The Professor gave me a series of lectures during my visits to his room in which he detailed for me the routines and the mechanisms of his untidy passions. He insisted during these long *études* that the most important piece of strategy was to get the subject to remove her shoes. 'Once the shoes are off, the battle is already half won,' he would say. 'Get a woman to walk around without shoes, without heels – she looks a fool, she feels a fool, she is a fool. Without her shoes, she is lost. Take the soft instep in your hand, caress her ankles, her calf, her knee – the rest is child's play. But remember, first off with the shoes.' While he talked, he would scratch his cat, which was part Siamese. The lecture was followed by a display of the collection of photographs he himself had taken, as evidence of the soundness of his theories.

When the Russian Ballet came to town, Professor Gorylescu was not to be had for any parties at the hotel. He went to all the performances, matinées and evenings alike and he hummed then the music of 'Puppenfee', 'L'Après-Midi d'un Faune', and the various *divertissements*, and was completely broke. One day he was in a state of the highest elation because he had invited a ballet-dancer to tea. He wanted me to come, too, because she had a friend, who would be an extra girl for me; both of them were exquisite creatures, he assured me, and I was to bring some tea, *marrons glacés*, *petits fours*, and lady-fingers.

I came early and I brought everything. He darkened the room, lit a brass samovar, laid out some cigarettes, sliced some lemons, hid the rowing-machine under the studio couch, and with the Japanese silk screen divided the room into two separate camps. On one side was the couch, on the other the great chair. He buttoned his Russian blouse, blew his nose frequently, and hummed as he walked up and down. He brushed the cat and put away a Spanish costume doll that might have made his couch crowded. He arranged the *petits fours* in saucers, and when the bell rang four times short and one long, he put a Chopin record on his victrola. 'Remember about the shoes,' he told me over his shoulder, 'and always play Chopin for ballet-dancers.' He quickly surveyed the room once more, turned on the bazaar lamp, and, humming, opened the door – and then stopped humming suddenly. He had invited two of the dancers, but up the stairs came a bouquet of girls, more than a dozen of them.

All at once it was the month of May in the dimmed room. The lovely guests complimented the samovar, the cat, the music, and the view from the balcony, to which they had opened the door, letting much fresh air come in, which intensified the new mood. Gorylescu's voice became metallic with introductions; he ran downstairs to get more glasses for tea and came back breathing heavily. All the girls, without being asked, took their shoes off immediately, explaining that their feet hurt from dancing. They arranged the shoes in an orderly row, as one does on entering a Japanese house or a mosque, then sat down on the floor in a circle. One of them even removed her stockings and put some slices of lemon between her toes. 'Ah-h-h,' she said.

There started after this a bewildering and alien conversation, a remote, foggy ritual, like a Shinto ceremonial. It consisted of the telling of ballet stories, and seemed to me a high, wild flight into a world closed to the outsider. The stories were told over and over until every detail was correct. In all of these stories appeared Anna Pavlova, who was referred to as 'Madame' – what Madame had said, what Madame had done, what she had thought, what she had worn, how she had danced. There was an atmosphere of furious backstage patriotism. The teller of each story swayed and danced with hands, shoulders, and face. Every word was illustrated; for anything mentioned – colour, light, time, and person – there was a surprisingly expressive and fitting gesture. The talker was rewarded with applause, with requests for repetition of this or that part again and again, and there swept over the group of girls waves of intimate, fervent emotion.

The Professor served tea on his hands and knees and retired to the shadows of his room. He sat for a while in the great chair like a bird with a wounded wing, and then with his sagging and cumbersome gait, he wandered around the group of innocents, who sat straight as so many candles, all with their shoes off. The room was alive with young heads and throats and flanks.

The Professor succeeded finally in putting his head into the lap of the tallest, the most racy of the nymphs. She quickly kissed him, said, 'Sh-h-h-h, daaaahrling,' and then caressed his features, the terrible nose, the eyebrows, the corrugated temples, and the great hands, with the professional detachment of a masseuse, while she related an episode in Cairo during a performance of *Giselle* when the apparatus that carried Pavlova up out of her grave to her lover got stuck halfway, and how Madame had cursed and what she had said after the performance and to whom she had said it. An indignant fire burned in all the narrowed eyes of the disciples as she talked.

Suddenly one of them looked at her watch, remembered a rehearsal, and the girls got up and remembered us. They all had Russian names, but all of them were English, as most ballet-dancers are; in their best accents, they said their adieus. With individual graces, they arranged their hair, slipped into their shoes, and thanked Maurice. Each one of them said 'Daaaahrling' to us and to each other. It was Madame Pavlova's form of address and her pronunciation.

All the girls kissed us, and it was as if we all had grown up in the same garden, as if they were all our sisters. The Professor said a few mouthfuls of gallant compliments, and when they were gone he fished the rowing-machine out from under the couch, without a word, and carried it in back of the Japanese screen. Together, we rearranged the room. The *marrons glacés* and the lady-fingers were all gone, but the cigarettes were still there.

XI

The Magician Does a New Trick

One day Professor Gorylescu came to see me at the banquet office. He hung his cane on the door-knob as usual, skimmed again through the reservation book, and asked me if I knew anything about dogs. He wanted to get a dog, he said, and he had seen one he thought he might buy. It was in a shop on Forty-ninth Street only a few blocks from the hotel, and was very expensive. He wanted a dog because he had decided he could use one in his sleight-of-hand performances, and he wanted me to come with him and look at the one he had found and see if I thought it would be a good dog for that purpose.

I took down my hat, put on a coat to hide my uniform, and we walked to the pet store. The dog of Professor Gorylescu's choice was a toy griffon; he sat in a garden of excelsior in the shop window and at frequent intervals was half smothered under the pink-and-black bellies of some fox-terrier puppies who seemed to move always in an avalanche. His name, we learned, was Confetti. Between avalanches, Confetti would right himself and look thoughtfully at the floor, as if he were trying to figure something out. He did not want to play. The proprietor of the shop asked fifty dollars for him, and Gorylescu bought him for thirty-five, with a leash and collar thrown in.

We took Confetti to the hotel, and I gave him part of a dish of lamb hash which I had ordered for my lunch. He pushed the saucer under my desk, and clattered around with it, and the Professor went out to buy a currycomb, some dog biscuits, and a dish for food. Confetti came out from under the desk and I got acquainted with him. He was a weird dog. He had a loose coat somewhat like the plumage of a grouse and his four legs were stuck into him without much care for design. He walked sideways with a sort of hop. He looked a hundred years old, and a hundred years of worry were in the misery of his lips and eyes. The end of his tongue stuck out between his teeth, and when he wanted to show affection he exploded with the sounds of a bronchial catarrh. Freezing and jittery, full of little fears, suspicions, and nervous twinges, he seemed to me to be the perfect dog for a sorcerer. He was exactly suited to Gorylescu, and I was glad I had advised Gorylescu to buy him.

I saw Confetti again a few weeks later when Gorylescu asked me to come to his house. Gorylescu had taught Confetti the first simple tricks, and before showing them in public, he wanted a few friends to come and see how clever the little dog was and how fast he had learned his lessons. I took a bus up to his château country in the Seventies. The street scene seemed always the same, an identical arrangement of people and things. There was invariably at one end of the block a man walking a chow dog, at the other end a woman carrying a hatbox, and between the two a Wanamaker truck, with two men carrying a couch either into a house or out of it. In the Hudson, sometimes, was a battleship. I went to the door of Gorylescu's castle and rang the bell. Mrs Houlberg stood at the window, as always, looking out into the street with one hand held diagonally across her face.

Gorylescu had not come in yet, and I sat in the entrance hall of the house and waited for him. Mrs Houlberg told me why she always looked out into the street. It was, she said, on account of her husband. He suffered from a serious heart condition, and she waited for him in fear every evening, worried that he might not come home, or, if he did, that people would be carrying him. He kept a card in the outer pocket of his coat on which she had lettered instructions where to bring him in

case he was suddenly stricken. As she spoke, she turned her
face in my direction only for brief moments, keeping her eyes
the rest of the time on the street outside.

'He'll go,' she said, and snapped her thin fingers. 'He'll go
just like that. One day they'll carry him in here – dead.'

Mr Houlberg, I learned, had a button-and-ribbon business
somewhere in back of Lord & Taylor's, and he worked too
hard.

Mrs Houlberg did not approve of Gorylescu's way of living.
He had too many girls, she said. She needed his rent money
badly or she would long ago have asked him to move out. She
said that the visits of women all day long, and at late hours
even, gave the house a bad name. As she spoke, the door opened
and a girl with a small bag came in and went upstairs without
saying anything. 'That's what I mean,' said Mrs Houlberg,
nodding at the girl's back. 'That's one of them. That's the latest
one. She has a key and she's going up to his room now.' The
girl was young, had a run in one of her stockings, nice legs,
thick lips, and blue-black hair. Polish, I thought – perhaps
from Scranton.

As for the dog, Mrs Houlberg liked dogs, she said, and she
did not mind feeding Confetti. But she wished that Gorylescu
would keep him upstairs. Ever since the Professor had brought
him down and shown him off, Mr Houlberg and the little dog
had been inseparable friends. They played together, the man
at the risk of his life. 'He's not supposed to bend over or run
up and down the stairs,' she said. 'He's supposed to sit still and

be quiet and not get excited. There he comes now,' she said, and opened the door.

Mr Houlberg looked as I feared he would. He sat down and asked how Confetti was, and then he leaned back and looked at the ceiling with his mouth open.

The Professor, who had been out airing Confetti, came in a moment later, and Confetti ran to Mr Houlberg as soon as he saw him, hopped into his lap, licked his hands and tried to reach his face. Mr Houlberg petted him and talked to him in German. There is a curious phrase which all people who speak German use when talking to a dog. They say, *'Ja wo ist denn das Hunderl? Ja wo iss er denn? Ja wo iss er denn?'* This is repeated as long as the conversation lasts, and is altogether meaningless, the translation being, 'Where is the little dog? Where is he? Where is he?' This goes on while the little dog sits right in front of them. Mr Houlberg said it over and over, and then the Professor and Confetti and I went upstairs. The Professor kissed the hand of the Polish girl, who said she was Spanish, that her name was Mercedes, and that she was a dancer. Two more friends of the Professor's came in – a theatrical agent and a man from a magicians' supply house – and the Professor got ready for his performance.

He went back of a Japanese screen and put on a tailcoat, a garment especially made for his act with Confetti. It had trick pockets all over it, big enough for Confetti to get into. The performance went very smoothly. Confetti disappeared slowly and came back again. Then he disappeared fast, both from in front and in back of the Professor and while the Professor was sitting, reclining, walking, standing, or turning around. The dog folded himself up silently and went into a pocket under the lapel or into one in the tails of the dress coat. After that was over, the Professor asked Confetti questions on international affairs, on the marital problems of movie stars, and even on what the future held for various politicians in the highest offices. Confetti answered with a nod of the head for 'Yes' and shook his head for 'No'. The Professor explained that he was trying to teach him to shrug his shoulders in answer to the more delicate questions.

After the performance the little dog hissed and coughed and scratched the floor, bowing to our applause. Then the Professor said good-bye to all of us except the Spanish dancer, and as we left Confetti squeezed out of the door and ran downstairs to his friend Mr Houlberg. He had smelled *Sauerbraten* and was going to get some.

A few days after all this, Gorylescu took the dog with him to Florida. He had made arrangements to appear with Confetti and an orchestra at some night club in Palm Beach. He came back to New York at the end of the season and stopped by the hotel as soon as he got off the train. We had written to him about an important engagement for the day after his return, and he now asked double the price he formerly got, and said that half of his fee was for Confetti, who was a sensation. He asked me to come along to his house and see for myself.

As we went out through the lobby of the Splendide, he waved to a girl who was waiting there, the dog in her arm. It was the Spanish dancer. She came along with us. Outside was a taxi with a theatrical trunk strapped on the back, a trunk, Gorylescu explained, that he never let out of his sight.

'Never take a dog to Florida,' the Professor said to us on the way uptown, 'on account of ticks. It's full of ticks down there. Look at him, he's full of them.' Confetti scratched himself all the way up to the Riverside Drive castle.

For once, Mrs Houlberg was not at the window. We went upstairs, all of us helping to carry the trunk. The Professor unlocked the door to his room, quickly looked through the accumulated mail, sorted letters from bills, and sniffed at several of the smaller envelopes. The girl silently unpacked the trunk. First she took out a collapsible chair that had a box under the seat instead of legs. Next she produced a nest of black-and-gold Chinese lacquer boxes. Then she laid out some tiny black garments which turned out to be full evening dress for Confetti.

While the Professor dressed the dog, he explained the routine. The first trick, he said, went like this: On one side of the stage, or the room, the dog sits on a chair facing the audience. On the other side stands the Professor. He asks a lady in the audience for the loan of a diamond bracelet. 'One, two, three,' and the bracelet is gone. Next, 'One, two, three' – the dog is gone. An attendant brings in a Chinese lacquer box, gold and black. The Professor opens it. Inside is a smaller box, inside that another one, and in the third box, unharmed and wearing the diamond bracelet around his neck, is Confetti.

'Now watch it closely,' said the Professor. He buttoned a high collar around Confetti's neck. The dog pulled his mouth sideways in annoyance, sneezed, and then tried to get some comfort by turning his head from side to side. Standing behind him, the Professor made a neat knot in the white tie under the dog's chin. 'Now,' he said, 'watch it closely!'

Confetti sat on his chair facing us. There was no bracelet, so the girl gave the Professor her wrist-watch instead. 'One, two, three,' the Professor said, and the wrist-watch was gone. Then 'Fffft' – the dog disappeared. The girl brought in the Chinese boxes and put them on the chair. Then she sat down beside me and chewed gum. 'Now watch me closely,' said the Professor, and he took out the first box, then the second. Then he smiled, raised his eyebrows to a high degree of fake surprise, and reached into the last of the small boxes. His face changed suddenly and he was really surprised now. The girl stopped chewing. The box was empty. No dog, no wrist-watch.

The Professor started several sentences of alarm and explanation while he looked behind the Japanese screen, under the couch, and into the trapdoor that was built into the chair. Having searched the room, he went out into the hall to whistle for the dog. On the stairs he saw the wrist-watch, and now he knew where Confetti was – down looking for his friend Mr Houlberg.

We went down to the basement, where the Houlbergs lived. The place smelled of flowers, there was a shabby palm in the hallway, and from the Houlbergs' parlour shone an uncertain, flickering light. It was the light of candles. The mourners sat in a circle which was open towards the door, and in a casket, as his wife so often had predicted, lay Mr Houlberg. The little dog, in his dress suit, sat behind a row of relatives, all properly dressed in black.

Just as we came up to the door, Mrs Houlberg saw the dog. She picked up Confetti and threw him at Gorylescu.

'You have a sense of humour all your own,' she said with a dry throat, and then she screamed, 'Get out! Get out!' the way bad actresses scream in rotten plays.

XII

The Dreams of the Magician

During the week of the Horse Show, a prominent Philadelphian who was a lover of horses always invited about fifty people to a supper in one of the private dining-rooms of the Hotel Splendide. The table for these suppers was always set up in the shape of a horseshoe; rows of miniature horses stood in the centre of the table, instead of flowers; the dishes were named after hunters and jumpers; the walls were draped in the stable colours of the host; and the waiters were dressed as grooms. There was an orchestra, but no dancing. Professor Gorylescu, the magician, came late in the evening to entertain the guests. He read their minds, and discovered that their thoughts were mostly on things equestrian; he also sat and looked into ladies' palms, and his findings again had to do with horses. Then he did some of his routine tricks, and the patter with which he accompanied them was filled with reference to turf, tack room, and famous mares and stallions. He worked hard on that night every year. The Philadelphian was extremely generous, never asked for a check, and just handed him several large bills.

At the end of the long performance, Professor Gorylescu always went into a little parlour off the dining-room, which was panelled and dimly lit, and there gave himself up to a large *fauteuil*. He fell into it, asked a passing waiter for a glass of water, loosened his black tie, opened his collar, and then covered his grey face with a large batik handkerchief. His hands, too large even for his immense body, hung down to the floor; his legs were folded one under the other and limp. The silken cloth alone was animated. It blew away from his face in the shape of a parachute and then, when he took in air, it came back and settled again, outlining for a moment the low, wedged forehead, the high cheekbones, the massive jaw with its bad teeth, and the obscene nose of the magician.

I knew the pose well, because I usually sat in another chair in a corner of the room. As assistant manager in the banquet department, I supervised the serving of the supper at these parties, and afterwards went to the little parlour to have my own supper. The waiter who looked after me moved about very quietly, so as not to disturb the magician; he walked on his toes, and I tried to keep knife and fork and wine-glass quiet. After I had my coffee I sank back in my chair also, and sometimes I talked, and the magician, under his handkerchief, drowsily responded. He was very much interested in society, in women and their pedigrees; he knew all the marriages and divorces, and he read Cholly Knickerbocker's writings faithfully, daily and Sunday.

We talked of these things, and he remained in a semi-comatose state for about half an hour. When he came out of it he looked as if he were having a chill, complained of pressure in his head, and started an absent-minded search for his hat, coat, and cane. Then he asked a waiter to show him where the *petits fours* were. With his hat on the back of his head and his cane hung over an arm, he followed the waiter to the buffet. Then he took the largest silver tray he found there and tilted it. The small pastries, cookies, and *mille-feuilles*, the bonbons, almonds, and nougat bars rolled into his open hand, and he put them in the outside pocket of his overcoat just as they were, without paper or other covering. Then he picked up from another tray a few more, to eat on the way down to the street.

To this annual supper one year came a close relative of the Philadelphia horseman and host – a distinguished-looking, dried-out old lady in black lace, who lived in a suite at the Splendide. With her came her psychoanalyst, Dr Desidir

Munkaczi, for she never went anywhere without him. He was a Hungarian Viennese who talked aggressively, leaving his mouth open between sentences and staring at people with rude intensity. He talked of his work, his travels, the mysteries of the mind, his cures, and of the desperate cases on which everyone had failed but Dr Desidir Munkaczi. He took a double serving of the dessert. Between mouthfuls of ice-cream he shot abrupt, courtroom-like questions across the table, pointed an accusing finger, leaned back, scared people, and enjoyed poking into their mental discomforts. He gave a show that was quite as good as the performance Professor Gorylescu was about to give, and he was being much better paid for it. He lived in a suite adjoining that of the old lady who was his steady patient, drove a large Lincoln with an aluminium body, and smoked the best cigars, and for all this the old lady had to pay, so that she could go about the city with him occasionally without fearing that the high buildings would fall down on her. This particular anxiety seemed to be her main trouble; she entered an elevator shaking all over, afraid of catastrophe, and never did she look out of a window except when leaning on the arm of Dr Munkaczi, who talked to her softly all the while.

At that year's supper-party Dr Desidir Munkaczi munched the last bit of icing off his second soufflé Alaska and watched with suspicion the performance of Professor Gorylescu. He tried to trip up the Professor several times, always without success. He gave him difficult thoughts to read, and at the end he said aloud and to everyone that this man was fabulous, a phenomenon of the first order, and that he had never seen or heard anything like it. As soon as the magician had left the room, Dr Munkaczi called to me as I went by his place at the table and said that he would like to have a few words with the man later on. I showed Dr Munkaczi where Professor Gorylescu would be resting for the next half-hour, and then went to have my supper in the corner of the little parlour. I had just had my coffee and was lying back in my chair, listening to the Professor breathing under his handkerchief, when Dr Munkaczi came into the room and asked in a whisper where the Professor had gone. I pointed at the handkerchief, which was rising and falling as usual. Walking on tiptoe, Dr Munkaczi turned out the lamps on the wall bracket in the room and left only one small, frosted table lamp burning. He pulled a chair across the carpet and sat down, carefully, silently, next to the Professor. He then announced his presence to him with a small cough, and said, 'This is Dr Munkaczi.' He took hold of one of the heavy hands hanging close to the floor, lifted it up, and told the Professor softly to stay quiet, to relax, to remain exactly as he was. After a while he said to the Professor, 'Tell me what comes into your mind. Just tell me what you are thinking about as the thoughts go through your mind.'

'Horses,' said the Professor, under the handkerchief.

'Horses? A lot of horses or just one horse, a particular horse?'

'A horse, a very particular horse.'

'You're fond of horses?'

'No. I hate horses – that is, I dislike them.'

'Have you had trouble with a horse?'

'No.'

'Where is this horse you are thinking about?'

'The horse is nowhere. This isn't a real horse. This horse is in a dream.'

'Oh,' said Dr Munkaczi, and then, 'Go on.'

'I dream of this horse—'

'You dream of this horse frequently?'

'Yes. Every night, almost, I dream of this horse, and I am very tired the next day.'

'Ah,' said Dr Munkaczi, '*zoologica erotica*.'

'I am tired,' said the Professor, 'because I have to run after the horse in that dream, and when I wake up I am so tired, so deadly tired! I run after the horse all night in these dreams.'

Dr Munkaczi moved his chair closer and he asked the Professor to tell him the dream from beginning to end.

'It differs,' said the Professor. 'It changes in many ways. It is never exactly the same. It varies, for example, with the seasons. Events – such as the Horse Show, the ballet, a personal experience – influence it, but it is always the same horse and the same woman.'

'A woman?'

'Yes, a woman, a beautiful woman about thirty-five years old sitting on the horse, astride. The horse is very wide – I must first tell you that I am happy only in the society of beautiful women,' added the Professor.

'Go on,' said Dr Munkaczi.

'I don't know just where to begin. I go home, I fall asleep after a night like this, and then it starts. Suddenly the horse is there. It stands there fat and wonderful, and it has human skin, not pink, not white, a little more rosy around the belly and on its flanks. The skin is fine, like marzipan, like the faultless complexion of a beautiful woman. On the horse sits the woman, the hair down her back. As a rule she is nude, only sometimes – I will explain this later – she wears clothes. She wears wonderful, exquisite clothes such as I have never seen in a store or at the parties I go to. They are more like costumes. I dream that I have sent them to her – I must also explain to you that I never can refuse women anything. I am about fifty years old.

'Well, she is a voluptuous woman with round, well-formed haunches, pink skin – but much finer, more transparent than the horse's – and very, very small hands. Her feet are lovely and they are not shod. She has hair that is as golden as the draperies in this room next door, rich and heavy, but I think I have told you that. And she is chaste – somehow I know that – and faithful. She looks at me awhile and then she waves her arms – soft, pliant arms – and one small rosy finger crooks and beckons me, and her lips say in a whisper, "Come, come," and then she gallops away, and I have to run after her.

'Oh, I have to tell you,' the Professor went on, 'that after these dreams became a steady occurrence I went to the trouble of taking riding lessons. I have told you that I detest horses. I am also afraid of them, but I thought then perhaps the dream would become more tolerable, that she might let me ride with her on the same horse, or that I might have one of my own and chase along.'

'Never works,' said Dr Munkaczi. 'Go on.'

'Now I run after her. In the spring we run through valleys filled with plants such as one finds only in the windows of florists and in botanical gardens. These and expensive shrubbery stand in carpets of flowers. The aroma of each flower is as strong as the smell of smoke or brandy. There are rivers and hills, and sheep mirror themselves as small clouds above in the sky. The sun is pink.

'In the autumn we run and jump over felled trees and the air smells of burnt leaves. The branches of the shrubs stand sideways in the wind; the clouds are shredded; there is much brown, red, and yellow; and occasionally a furry animal runs by. Music like Wagner, but not so loud, is always in this dream. And then comes winter. Oh, the cold, cold winter!

'The sun is small as a dime, and blue. The horse arrives in furs — in ermine, in sable — and under this it has a fur of its own. I ran my hand over it one night; it was covered by a short-haired, stiff coat of its own fur, such as closely cropped velvet, like the arm of this chair. I got much pleasure from it, but it ran away. I heard the woman's voice far away in the wind. Then I saw her and she turned and beckoned, but there was ice everywhere, and water rippled beneath it. It sounded everywhere as if someone were dropping pearls on a mirror. In these icy dreams all the echoes are like the crackling of thin glass. I am a coward then, afraid to cross the ice. I bleed out of small wounds and almost awaken; but then, far away at the end, near her, a bolt of red cloth unrolls itself; it grows as it comes to me across the ice, and on this I run to her, in a glassy din, in the shrill breaking of ice all around me.'

The Professor scratched himself under his arm. Munkaczi went to the door, and looked after his old lady patient for a few moments, and then came back and sat down again.

'I dream best when the ballet is in town,' continued the Professor. 'I must tell you that I am very fond of ballet-dancers. When the ballet is here, then the horse has long veils at its side, like a goldfish. There is a carmine curtain left and right, and there are trees pasted on netting; the nets are hung with expensive trinkets. In a lambent light she rides, and then she wears a costume, something like a tricos, impossible to describe – silver-and-white plumage painted on black velvet. There is fine music far away, tinkling, like wind playing in a crystal chandelier. She rides then and the horse dances. But again she turns and beckons to me, and at the back of the stage she stops at a brook and she leaves her clothes there. I find the dresses and I steal them and kiss them.'

'Hmm, *faute de mieux*,' said Dr Munkaczi.

Professor Gorylescu removed the silk handkerchief and blinked.

The Doctor then proceeded with an outline for a cure. He suggested ten treatments, for which he said he would make no charge. He advised the Professor to seek more the society of ladies if he could manage it, advised regular hydrotherapy and plenty of open-air exercise.

I did not see the Professor again until about a month later, in the first days of winter. There was a party at a private residence on upper Fifth Avenue, and the catering department of the Splendide took care of the service. I was sent there to look after things, and the Professor turned up as the entertainer. After his performance he rested in the library of the house. He fell asleep, his lap filled with pastry crumbs, and when he woke up it was almost daylight and the party was over. The musicians were packing their instruments and the waiters were putting away the unused linen in large baskets. Professor Gorylescu and I left the house together. He headed for the Park. He said that he exercised frequently, ate vegetables and drank milk, and took long walks and cold baths. 'This performance tonight should have almost killed me,' he said, and pushed his hair out of his face and under his hat. 'I must have read a hundred minds, but I don't feel a bit tired. I walk in the Park every morning,' he went on, and stretched his neck. 'This diet, the exercises' – he waved his arms – 'these treatments of Dr Munkaczi have done wonders for me. I sleep well. I am a new man.' He whistled and jumped over a bench.

We turned up the Avenue and came to the new Savoy-Plaza Hotel. It stood gleaming in its white tile. A man was polishing a stand-pipe next to the door; a milk-wagon horse slid and skated out of Fifty-ninth Street. General Sherman on his golden horse reflected the first sun-rays, and the nude atop the fountain made everything seem doubly cold. All the branches on the young trees around the fountain were behung with icicles; they looked like chandeliers; some shone red and green where the traffic-lights were reflected in them. We walked on. In the Zoo's outdoor cages vapour rose from the nostrils of bison, zebras, and llamas, and around a turn of the bridle-path appeared a blonde woman, hatless, astride a fat bay gelding. She had a good seat. She was soft and round and had rosy cheeks, and when she came near I saw it was the former Julia Coutts Burmeister – a girl who had come out at the Splendide the winter before and to whom Cholly Knickerbocker had referred as a Grade C debutante, because her money came from St Louis beer. She had married since.

The Professor and I had both been at the coming-out party and at the wedding supper some months afterwards, and she seemed to recognise us. At any rate, she smiled at us and waved. It was so much like one of the Professor's dreams that I thought he would have to start running after the horse. But he only stuck his obscene nose into the air and tried to think of her husband's name. He relaxed and his body slumped for a moment, but then he stuck out his chest and straightened up. He took a few high jumps in the air, beat himself with his arms, made a snowball, and threw it at a tree. 'Hollister – Hohlwein – Hohl – Hollstein,' he said. 'Hollstein is her husband's name.' He took a bonbon from his pocket and fed it to a squirrel. He was obviously completely cured.

XIII

My Valet Lustgarten

The management of the Splendide felt that all its employees must be carefully dressed. The uniforms for the bellboys and footmen, the doormen and elevator operators were supplied by the house at a cost of tens of thousands of dollars in tailoring and in upkeep. The executives were fashion plates and most of the *maîtres d'hôtel* had their clothes made in London.

Dress was most important in the banquet department. The functions that took place there – weddings, balls, diplomatic dinners, concerts, coming-out parties – demanded that the permanent staff present an elegant appearance.

Clothes had not only to be of fine cut and the latest fashion; they had also to be forever pressed, the boots shined, the linen fresh.

During the season there was only a brief time, while the guests of one party were leaving and before those of the next arrived, for going upstairs to dress. We changed four or five times a day – from morning coat to cutaway, to dinner coat, to tails, and always in a hurry. The worry about having enough clean linen, the fiddling with buttons, cuff-links, and studs, pulling them out of one shirt and sticking them into the starchy-edged holes of the bosoms and cuffs of a new one, taking trees out of one pair of shoes to put them into another, looking for white waistcoats, was annoying; so was putting on high collars, tying thin cravats into bows, with nervous fingers, sometimes three times during a long night.

The cleaning and pressing of clothes was attended to by the house valets. Each of them was assigned to a floor of the hotel, to attend the guests, and they were supposed to come down in the afternoon to do some hurried pressing and cleaning for the staff, for which they were paid by the hotel. They were all English valets, and they felt it to be beneath their dignity to look after us; they gave us the most hurried, careless service possible. They would never bother to lay out our clothes, or put studs and cuff-links into shirts, and of course we could not expect them to be there in the middle of the night when we needed them most. We tried several other arrangements, such as having a bus boy take the things to an outside tailor and trying to train him to arrange the studs, but they all had fat dirty fingers or were clumsy, and sometimes the clothes did not come back in time, and it never worked out right. It was a mess until I found Joseph Lustgarten.

One afternoon, when there was only a lecture in one of the smaller ballrooms and no dinner scheduled for the evening, I left an old waiter in charge and went for a ride in the Hispano. One of the ballet-dancers I had met at Gorylescu's tea-party, named Lydia, went along.

We drove up Riverside Drive and onto the Dyckman Street ferry. On this ferry-boat was a musician, and after the engines started pounding and the boat had left its slip, he began to play on a three-quarter violin. The weather had worn all the patina off his instrument; it looked as if it had been sand-papered. In the bad light of the gangway in which the car stood, the man's threadbare overcoat, the fiddle, the face, the hat, and the patched shoes, were all one colour – a dull green. The thin fingers were blue, and they walked up and down over the strings like the legs of a bug. There was a drop on the end of the man's nose. It was cold and windy. He played Kreisler's 'Liebesleid' – he played it very correctly, and Lydia said how surprising this was. She knew the music – she had danced to the melody – and she said he played it without any melancholic liberties, without the usual whining. He came to the car after he had ended the 'Liebesleid', and I gave him a bill.

He took it and walked to the edge of the ferry-boat and unfolded the bill; it was a five-dollar bill. He folded it carefully – unbuttoned the overcoat, another coat, pushed a sweater up and then slid the bill into the pocket of his vest. Then he looked at the river, at Lydia, and again at the Hispano and at me, and I felt that it was wrong to have given him the bill, that it would have been better just to have given him a quarter. I was upset because the man seemed very unhappy about it; he fingered his instrument and blew warm air on his hands.

I got out and spoke to him. He clicked his heels and made a bow and he told me that he was not a professional musician, but a tailor out of work; that he came from Graz, and had served in a Viennese regiment, where he had been orderly to a colonel, who was a baron. His conversation was still infected with this experience. When I spoke to him in German, he answered in precise military language somewhat softened by his Austrian dialect. He addressed me by several titles – '*Ja, Herr Graf, jawohl, Herr Baron*' – and when I asked him to play some *Heurigen* music, he again clicked his heels, wiped his nose on his sleeve, and said, '*Zu Befehl, Exzellenz.*'

Here stood the complete solution to our valet problem. When he finished playing 'Sweet Rosmarin', I told him to get into the car. He protested, but when I promised him a job, he sat down gingerly on the leopard skins in the back. We covered him up with a rug, and he ate with us at West Point. The next day he reported at the hotel. His name was Lustgarten, 'Joseph Lustgarten, Your Excellency,' he said, and stood at attention.

Lustgarten was immediately engaged to press and take care of our clothes, lay out the linen, shine the shoes. He ate in the hotel and helped out with other work on occasion. He made good money, and von Kyling, the director of the banquet department, gave him a cast-off cutaway and striped trousers. Others gave him a dinner coat and civilian suits; and it turned out that my old shoes fitted him. After he was properly dressed and warm, his white hair combed, he looked very distinguished and historic, like Metternich.

I soon found out why he had appeared to be so upset on the ferry-boat. There was a contradiction between the expression on his face and the emotions he felt. When he was happiest – and the five-dollar bill had made him very happy – he looked as other people do when they cut themselves or swallow something bitter. His laugh was a string of indrawn muted cries, and the more he laughed the sadder he seemed.

He had an annoying habit, when nervous, of pulling his fingers out of their joints and snapping them back again, but otherwise he was without fault. He was happy with his job, never tired, needed no sleep, was full of warm little talk and restful. He had a quiet, kindly humour, and he loved to read.

We all had dressing-rooms in one of the noisy sections of the hotel. When we worked very late it was our privilege to ask at the desk for a room to sleep in; during the season we worked late almost every night and never left the hotel for weeks at a time. The room clerk would give us the key to a vacant suite – the Splendide had no single rooms – and, in return for some cigarettes or an occasional bottle of wine, he saw to it that the rooms were the best and that we were not disturbed the next morning. We got to bed about four or five, sometimes six in the morning. When the exciting parties ended, the music seemed to keep on playing – the bass fiddles and the big drums beat on and on, and I rarely got more than two hours' sleep.

At about midnight Lustgarten would go to the front office and get the key to the room where I was to sleep. Then he packed the clothes for the next day – the linen, the shoes, the tie, toilet articles, and pyjamas – into a black bag. From one party or another there was always champagne and caviar left over. He would put some caviar in a dish with ice, take a bottle of stale leftover champagne, a toaster, and bread. After plugging in the toaster and cooling the wine, he sat and waited for me.

We were in a different room every night, but every night we ate caviar. I ate it in bed with a soup-spoon, drank champagne, and wrote plays. At that time I wanted to be a playwright. Lustgarten read my manuscripts back to me. I wrote about one play a week. None of them seemed very good. I never could let go of a character. There were always two of them – a good one who was dumb; a bad one who was intelligent. The dumb one began by asking the other a question, and then the other answered for an hour. Lustgarten sat on the edge of my bed and gave me the day's accumulated scandal about the hotel guests and employees. He darned socks, bit off thread, sewed on buttons, and whistled Viennese music. He slept on a divan in the living-room.

There came several nights when the hotel was filled and no room was available for us except the Adam Suite. This apartment was the quintessence of elegance. It was leased by a multi-millionaire, and was on the highest floor of the hotel; its ceilings were sixteen feet high, the furniture museum pieces. On a small dais in one bedroom stood a canopied Napoleon bed. The bath was sunken, the fixtures gilded. There were Aubusson carpets and tapestries in the living-room. The silver, the glasses, the china in the dining-room were all antique and priceless. The library held first editions and fine bindings, also a Bechstein piano, on which stood a group of photographs – among them Queen Marie of Rumania, two members of the British royal family, Mary Pickford, and Bernard Shaw. All the photographs were signed, and some had a few words of friendship added. The tenant of the Adam Suite was in Europe most of the time, in the care of a specialist. He travelled with a doctor and two nurses from Baden-Baden to Bad Gastein to Paris. The Suite stood empty the better part of the year.

We moved in very carefully at first. Every night Lustgarten packed the little black bag, and every morning he brought it down to the ballroom again. When the room clerk, after a gift of a box of cigars, said that it was all right to stay there, Lustgarten at first left only our tooth-brushes and the packed bag. But eventually, when I came in after a party one night,

I found all my clothes hanging in the closet. Lustgarten clicked his heels, said, '*Zu Befehl, Exzellenz*,' and established us there for good. It was better for him, too, because there was a second bedroom and a bath, and a pantry where he could keep cold food, a few bottles of wine and cold meats, sturgeon and other leftovers, and the caviar.

Lustgarten now bloomed into the perfect servant. He not only put buttons and cuff-links into the shirts, mended socks, and shined boots, he knew remedies for sore throat, tired eyes, hangovers. He always arranged his face into agreement; he played nice music; looked out of the window in the morning and announced the weather, always with consideration – 'A very nice rainy day, Your Excellency,' he said. 'Just a little wind, a lovely high wind.' He never wanted a day off. We often went to the theatre together; we saw most of Eugene O'Neill that way, 'You write much better, *Herr Baron*,' Joseph often said to me.

For six months we lived undisturbed in the Adam Suite. Lustgarten loved to sit on the floor and play the violin. Gorylescu, the magician, came up on Sunday evenings with his trained dog. Kalakobé visited us. I took up painting again, and the models joined us for little cold suppers and music on the violin and the Bechstein. When there was nothing else to do, there were two Renoirs and four Toulouse-Lautrecs to look at. In the library were Werfel and Thomas Mann in first editions, and Voltaire in the original text. And there were the millionaire's subscriptions to magazines: *Vanity Fair*, *La Vie*

Parisienne, *Life, Judge*, the *Atlantic Monthly*, *Punch*, the *Sphere*, the *Tatler*, *Simplicissimus*, and *Town Topics*.

One night I brought to the apartment a Bavarian who had been a cavalry major in the German Army. His troop had been stationed in Regensburg. His name was Count Hugo von Trautmansdorff, and he had known my grandfather well and had been a steady customer in my grandfather's brewery in Regensburg. He had come to America after the World War.

Lustgarten fell all over himself with attentions. For the first time he failed to call me *Herr Baron*, *Herr Exzellenz*, and *Herr Graf*. All his efforts were directed towards von Trautmansdorff. He followed the Count all over the apartment while von Trautmansdorff looked at the Bonaparte bed and the Toulouse-Lautrecs and the collections of photographs on the piano. When the Count had seen the whole apartment, Joseph settled him in a chair in the corner of the library, near a big window, where he could look out over the city. The Count told me that he still had some family jewels and a small income, but it was not enough so that he could live like a gentleman. To marry an American woman, he said, was a terrible way out, and it was probably impossible, since he was too old and had asthma. To do exhibition dancing was also impossible, for the same reason. His one hope, he said, was to have a little riding academy. It was that or good-bye, beautiful world. He got up then and stood for some time looking down at the street, which was thirty-six stories below.

From that time on I had trouble with Joseph. Although the season of balls and banquets was over and there ought to have been less work for him to do, he seemed always busy. The reason for this was that he broadened his activities and began soliciting business among the captains in the various restaurants, the room waiters, and all the employees who had anything to press or repair. Over the tub in his own bathroom he hung a long pole, and uniforms dangled from this, with tickets on the sleeves. He engaged a bus boy to work for him in his free hours, and the boy was continually rushing in and out of the apartment, hunched under pressed and unpressed uniforms. From the bathroom came the hissing of steam and the smell of moist clothes, and the apartment took on the odour of a tailor shop.

Lustgarten had no time to run errands for me or to sit on the edge of my bed and talk. He was too tired, or too busy, to play the violin or read my plays. He was so busy that he did not even go down to eat. His meal was a dreadful half-hour in the Adam Suite. At five o'clock in the afternoon he sent the bus boy out to a delicatessen on Third Avenue. When the boy arrived with a paper bag and a bottle of beer, Joseph turned his tailor's iron downside up and boiled himself two potatoes on it. He was fond of smoked herring, and especially a very fat kind that was imported from Germany and was called *Bückling*. With his pocket-knife he scraped the metallic skin off. Then he cut six slices of pumpernickel and smeared them thickly with Liederkranz. Next he covered the Liederkranz with chopped chives, and finally, when the potatoes were done, he opened the bottle of beer.

At the beginning of the meal he would lean on the Bechstein piano, look at the photographs and the distinguished signatures, and eat the herring very daintily, his lips pulled back from his teeth and his little finger stretched away from his hand. But when he came to the Liederkranz sandwiches he turned his back to the photographs to concentrate on his dessert, and his face took on its most bitter lines of happiness.

Eventually Joseph added Count von Trautmansdorff to his list of clients. The Count lived in a small furnished apartment on Sixtieth Street east of the Park, in a rooming-house filled with others like himself. He had *entrée* into the best society, and he used to dine out occasionally with the hope of getting someone interested in his riding academy. Beforehand he would bring his tailcoat up to the Adam Suite, and Lustgarten would work on it until it was wearable again.

When he and Lustgarten were together, it was like being around the stables of a cavalry regiment. They spoke of horses, drills, terrain, manoeuvres – the Count with telegraphic briefness, as if issuing commands; Lustgarten standing before him with his hands flat on the seams of his trousers, his face miserable with joy. In the late hours, Lustgarten would permit himself to sit down, and then he and the Count talked of ancient Hapsburg scandals: the *Affaire Mayerling*, the idiocies of the archdukes, and the mad Wittelsbachs. Fritzl, the bus boy, sat silent, his eyes wide. Occasionally he tried to get the conversation around to Regensburg, where he came from, but it didn't work. The Count detested Regensburg.

Until the pressing-shop was set up, Lustgarten had never given me any cause to complain, and I stood it a long while; but at last I told him that it would have to stop, that he would have to eat out in the pantry with the door closed, and that above all he would have to get rid of the smelly waiters' garments in his bathroom. He promised to do so.

One evening a few days later I came in and found the suite again smelling like a tavern. The bus boy rushed past me on his way out, and from the bathroom – fhhhs, fhhhs – came the sound of pressing. I opened the windows and called Lustgarten, and this time I spoke to him in anger. I had never spoken to him that way before. He smiled, and his servant's face became very tired. He tried to speak, and then after a moment he excused himself and left the room.

That night he packed quietly and left. In a day or so I had a letter from him, postmarked 'New York City'. It began, '*Sehr geehrter Herr und lieber Freund*,' and was full of Austrian misspelling of German words. He would never forget my many kindnesses, the letter said, and he would always look back upon this year as one of the happiest. He had been able to save up a little money, especially during the last few months, and as soon as the warm weather came, he and His Excellency, Count von Trautmansdorff, were going to open a riding academy in Central Park. They were only going to have two horses at first, but there would be more later, and they hoped to have my patronage.

The idyll of the Adam Suite came to an end soon after.

The millionaire to whom the suite was leased had written to the manager that he intended to give it up, to sublet it, if a suitable tenant could be found. Mr Brauhaus, the manager, had an inquiry for just such an apartment, and one morning, while I was still in bed, he showed the suite to two ladies.

An entire procession came into the living-room: Mr Brauhaus, the two ladies, Fassie, the assistant manager, and Madame de Brissonade, the housekeeper. They all stood at proper distances from each other, according to rank. The ladies inspected the furniture, the view, the layout, and asked questions.

Mespoulets, who stayed with me after Lustgarten left, came into the bedroom shaking all over. He looked at me as if I knew the solution to a great mystery, and he stammered that Jesus Christ was outside.

Mespoulets looked as if he were going to cry and hid behind a screen. The door was opened by the assistant manager, and when he saw someone asleep in the bed he said, 'Pardon me,' and closed it again. The visitors were ushered out of the apartment, but the assistant manager came back to the bedroom and walked over to the bed, and then he went out and got Mr Brauhaus. They talked in whispers because I was asleep. Fassie pointed to the champagne stand and the empty bottle. He lifted it out of the melted ice-water and fished out the label so that Mr Brauhaus could see that the wine was of good vintage.

'They are fine dogs,' Fassie said, hoarsely. 'The gentlemen of the banquet department, they know what they like.' He held up the empty box of caviar. 'Monsieur Louis here also drives a Hispano,' he added. He loved the 'fine dogs', and repeated it several times in describing the elegance with which we lived in the banquet department.

Mr Brauhaus looked very angry while he listened, but he told Fassie to let me sleep. He had read the report of the banquet the night before and seen that we had gone to bed at six in the morning. He agreed, however, that it was a little thick. Still whispering, he told the assistant to have me report to his office as soon as I woke up. 'Diss time I'll fire him, Gotdemn it, Cheeses Greisd,' he whispered, and carefully closed the door.

XIV

The Banquet

Chevalier had rendered street songs of Paris, among them a mildly obscene ballad about an elephant. The costliest wines had been served and the menu for the dinner for three hundred people was the best the kitchens of the Splendide could turn out. After a midnight supper of boars' hams, Polish hams, Virginia hams, wild turkeys, lobster claws, *pâté de foie gras*, and truffles – and after a breakfast served at four in the morning – the Irish scrub-women sat out on the backstairs drinking leftover champagne from glasses with which over-tired waiters had wobbled out into the pantry. The night electrician and the doorman leaned on pillars and waited to turn out the lights, hoping that the last guests would soon leave.

The last guests sat in one of the smaller apartments adjoining the large ballroom. They were all drunk, and the host was listening to Professor Gorylescu, who was telling his fortune. The host nodded with happy approval at the glowing picture that Gorylescu read from his hand and when it was over he leaned back into the soft pillows of the couch and told the story of his life. One of the guests was ill, holding on to a sideboard, and a houseman stood by and waited until he had done, to clean up the mess with sawdust and a small shovel. In the empty ballroom two people danced to an orchestra of sixty men, who continued to play in the ballroom, and the magician's dog, Confetti, lay under the *maître d'hôtel*'s desk and trembled.

In an hour the guests had left, and the magician had gone home without his dog. Mespoulets made a few sandwiches of sturgeon, smearing caviar over them, picked up the dog and a bottle of champagne, and the night electrician took us up in the elevator to the top floor of the hotel. This was while Mespoulets and I were still living in the Adam Suite.

Mespoulets took off his clothes and put on a nightshirt. He slipped into a cheap flannel robe and went into the library with his glass of wine. He had started to rearrange the books, and he sat on the floor now among stacks of them, which he had pulled from the shelves that covered two walls of the room. He had placed a lamp on the floor, next to where he sat.

He wore no slippers, and the small dog licked his toes while he built new stacks out of the books, mumbling, 'Biography American, biography literary, history, economics, politics.' He was furious at the carelessness with which the library had been arranged – sociology, drama, and poetry all thrown in together. He made sounds of disgust as he found *Don Quixote* in three editions mixed up with *The Mysteries of Paris*, Balzac, Lenin, *Wuthering Heights*, and *Wolfert's Roost*. Between *Conflict and Dream* and *The Meaning of Meaning* were several volumes of Dickens. Mumbling 'Fiction classical', he put Dickens aside and groaned.

Occasionally he opened a book and read in it, and when I called to him to ask whether Orpheus or Morpheus is the one who takes you into his arms to sleep, he said that it was Morpheus, and that Orpheus was the god of Music. He brought in Bulfinch's *Mythology* and went out again. The magician's dog had come with him and hopped on my bed.

Mespoulets said that he was not sleepy. An hour later, while I fed the dog small pieces of the sturgeon sandwich, he came in again with a small volume. 'Where have we heard this story before?' he said. He sat down at the edge of my bed and began to read from a story by Petronius, written in the year 57 after the birth of Christ.

TRIMALCHIO'S BANQUET

... After the fish was served, six poulards followed, and some grouse that were stuffed with stuffed eggs. Trimalchio begged us to do away with them, adding that they were easy to eat, that the larger of the birds were hens whose bones had been carefully pulled out. In the meantime, someone knocked at the door, and a guest, in ceremonial white robe, surrounded by a troupe of friends, entered.

I wanted to get up and walk toward them with bare feet, but Agamemnon laughed and said, 'Quiet, no fuss, it's only Habinnas, who is a tolerable sculptor and good at making the better sort of monuments.'

This gave me courage. I resumed my comfortable position and I watched Habinnas with great admiration. Habinnas, already drunk, rested his hands on the shoulders of his wife. His head was stuck into a wreath and from his eyes and ears ran melted salve; it ran from under the wreath down into his eyes. At last he went to the place of honour and asked for wine and warm water.

Trimalchio was delighted with Habinnas's happy mood. He called for a larger cup to drink out of and he asked Habinnas how he liked the banquet he had just come from.

'We had everything – only you were absent,' answered Habinnas. 'We celebrated most magnificently. Scissa was holding a great wake in honour of his dead slave – I estimate that he inherits a good deal from the dead servant. We had a wonderful time there, in spite of having to pour half the wine over the dead man's bones.'

'What did you have to eat?' asked Trimalchio.

'I will tell you if I can remember. I have such a good memory that sometimes I forget my own name. In spite of that, I think I remember that for the first course we had a pig; a pig covered with wreaths, surrounded by sausages, small birds, mangold, and black bread. I would rather eat black bread than white – it gives more power.

'The second dish was a cold pudding, covered with exquisite warm Spanish honey – I ate too little of the pudding, but of the honey I couldn't get enough. Of the pea and bean salad I took very little, and also of the fruits. I took a few apples along – here they are in my napkin – because if I don't bring something back to my favourite slave he will be in bad humour for days.

'My wife just reminds me that we were also served with the hind leg of a young boar, and my Scintilla here carelessly ate too much of it, and almost spat out her own lung and liver. I ate more than a pound of it myself – it tasted exactly like the dark meat of game. If the bear eats the man, I said to myself, how much more must the man eat the bear—

'Afterwards we had some soft cheese, a wine soup, snails, a ragout, liver, more stuffed eggs, and mustard – and all of it served in large round dishes, for which praise be to Palamedes, who invented them. Following this, oysters were passed, and everyone reached for them. The boar's ham came back, but we sent it away—'

... Fortunata came in, her dress held high by a yellow belt, so high that her cherry-coloured underclothes were exposed. The silver ribbons that held the gold-embroidered shoes to her small feet shone, and a carmine cloth hung at her side on which she wiped her hands. She sat down on the cushion next to Scintilla, the wife of Habinnas. She kissed her, and Scintilla clapped her hands with joy, and said, with her eyes resting deeply in those of the other woman, 'Is it you? Is it really you at last?'

Later on Fortunata removed her golden bracelets and armbands and showed them to Scintilla. She also removed the heavy bands from her ankles, and finally her hair net, which she boasted was woven of the finest gold threads obtainable.

Trimalchio observed all this and he gave orders to bring the jewellery to him. When it was placed in a heap in front of his chair, he shouted: 'You see here – her anklets – six and a half pounds of gold; and this bracelet – ten pounds – that is how we fools allow them to rob us!' He insisted that one of the slaves bring in a scale so that everyone could see that he was not lying. He weighed all the jewellery, one piece after the other.

Scintilla was not to be outdone. She took a golden capsule off a heavy necklace and out of it she rolled the largest pearls that anyone at the table had ever seen. She gave them to Fortunata to look at. 'A gift from my beloved lord,' she said. 'No one on earth may own a better pair.'

'You lay in my ears and cried until I finally had to buy the cursed glass beads for you!' screamed Habinnas. 'You have almost made a beggar out of me on account of it. She wants to have them made into earrings! If I had a daughter I'd cut her ears off.'

'If women didn't exist,' said Trimalchio, 'we would consider all this as so much dirt – but now it is established as gold, a value as certain as the fact that we drink cold and piss warm.'

Mespoulets left the room for a moment; then returned and went on reading.

Trimalchio clapped his hands and ordered that the dessert be brought in. Slaves carried all the tables out and brought in smaller ones. They covered the dance floor with yellow and red sawdust.

An Alexandrian slave, who served basins of warm water as soon as the sweets were taken away, began to imitate the song of the nightingale, but Trimalchio waved him away impatiently and ordered another slave who sat at the feet of Habinnas to sing.

The boy sang:

'On the high sea of Aeneas –
With the fleet and the voyage certain …'

No tune was ever so amiss, no voice has ever torn my ears as
that youth's did. After this, the barbaric entertainer, at times
in high voice, at times in low, recited street songs – cheap
ballads, so that for the first time Virgil disgusted me. When
he finally became exhausted, Habinnas said to me, 'Isn't he
wonderful? All I have to do is send him to the market. That
is where he picks it up. He can imitate a mule driver or a
soldier. He is the cleverest boy I know. He is a shoemaker,
a cook, a baker; he is handy at everything. He has only two
faults. Without them he would be perfect. Occasionally he
goes out of his mind, and he snores at night. Of course, you
can see he is also cross-eyed. That he is cross-eyed makes
no difference – even Venus is – and in spite of it he sees
everything – and keeps it to himself. I bought him as a
one-eyed slave for a hundred talers.'

At that statement Scintilla interrupted him and said,
'You did not tell your friend that he is also the best procurer
in town.' And looking at the youth she said, 'Some day I'll
have a cross burned into your forehead, Cross-eyes – wait
and see if I don't.'

Trimalchio smiled and said, 'Don't be jealous, Scintilla
my dove. True as I am Trimalchio, when I served my erst-
while master I was no better.' The cross-eyed slave, as if
that were high praise and hope of future for him, pulled a
small flute from his cloth, and for more than half an hour
he played while Habinnas accompanied him, pulling on his
lower lip with his fingers and making a humming sound. It

was a tiresome performance and finally the youth stood up, walked to the centre of the floor with a whip, and imitated the mule drivers, an act which I had witnessed a dozen times. He did this until Habinnas called him, kissed him on the lips, and gave him his cup to drink out of. 'Good, good, very good,' he said to him. 'You shall have a pair of new shoes tomorrow.'

It was so dreary that I would have left and run away then and there, if a new dish had not come to the table. A round platter was brought in on which rested a substantial pie, made of larks, dried pigeons, and pickled nuts. It was followed by quinces into which cloves had been stuck, which made them look like porcupines. This all would have been sufficient to keep me there, but it was only the beginning of the new meal. After this came something for which I would have run for miles. It appeared to be a stuffed goose and around it, in a most appetising arrangement, lay all kinds of fish, birds, and fruits.

Trimalchio, keeping everyone's hands away from the dish, said, 'All that you see here is made out of one substance.'

I, who am the most experienced in such matters, said quietly to my neighbour, Agamemnon, 'It's very nice, but I hope it isn't made of dung. I have been witness to such a jest. In Rome, at the Saturnalia, I almost ate some of it.'

I had hardly, just to taste it, helped myself to a small apple, when Trimalchio stated that his cook, the smartest cook in the world, had made it all out of a pig. 'He is price-less,' said Trimalchio. 'Order him to do it and he makes a fish out of a sowbelly – out of lard he makes trees; he uses ham to manufacture turtledoves, and with a pork loin he imitates a chicken.'

Suddenly two slaves came into the room, loudly arguing. Each of them held several bottles, and after Trimalchio had settled their differences, they ignored him and broke each other's bottles. We were feeling surprised and shocked at the impertinence of the slaves, who seemed to be drunk, when suddenly we beheld all kinds of small mussels, sea urchins, shells, and snails rolling out of the broken bottles. It had all been an invention of the wonderful cook, and it was all made of paste, deliciously sweet. The two slaves picked the dessert off the floor and then passed it around in large golden vessels.

I am almost ashamed to tell the following: In the modern fashion, pretty slaves with long hair entered, carrying vases with perfumed lotions. With their small hands they applied the salve to the feet of the guests, to the soles, the heels, the ankles, the knees and the legs and the haunches. And afterwards they poured some of the lotion into the wine cups.

Fortunata wanted to dance, but Trimalchio now invited his servants to join us. A moment after this announcement there was hardly any room at the table. They almost pushed us on the floor. I will never forget the cook who made a

goose out of a pig. The stench of the whole kitchen and
the scullery came from him. He was not satisfied to lie
under the table, but crawled out and began to imitate
Thespis. He said that he had always wanted to be an actor.
He insisted on betting his master, later that evening, that
at the next games, wearing a green toga, he would carry
away the first prize, and then he fell asleep and smelled
of kitchen again.

In all this mess Trimalchio almost dissolved in pleasure.
'My friends!' he shouted. 'Aren't slaves human? Haven't
they taken women's milk exactly as we? Ah, what bitter
fate is theirs! But all the same, I will make things right for
them – as truly as I am alive, I shall see that they too will
breathe the fresh air – freely. In short, my friends, in my
testament, I shall set them free.

'I will begin with Fortunata. She shall be my chief
beneficiary, and I will recommend her to all my friends.

'All this I make public now so that my slaves shall love
me as much as if I had already passed away.'

Tearfully he then looked at Habinnas and said, 'What
do you think of it, good friend? Will you build me my
mausoleum the way I have ordered it? I beg of you, at the
feet of my statue put my little dog and the wreaths and my
scent bottles. Cut all this in the stone carefully and so that
no one may mistake it – and cut into it also all the battles
I have won. Up above, the tomb must be a hundred feet
wide, and below, two hundred. I want one of every sort of

tree planted around it. To make sure that no one defiles my last resting place, also carve a chair somewhere, in which one of my freed slaves shall sit and prevent the public from coming too close. I beg you also not to forget to have a ship with sails, the sails bulging in the wind. And I must sit in a judge's chair, in a purple gown, with five golden rings on my fingers. I must be shown throwing pieces of gold among the people. You know that I have given public banquets at which everyone who attended has been given two gold pieces. You may, if you wish, perhaps on another side of the tomb, picture the banquet hall, and in it show the people and how happy they are. At my right in this scene, you may place Fortunata. Place her to my right, be sure, with a dove in her hand, and the small dog at her feet. Make her sad, perhaps looking at an urn, a broken urn on which a weeping youth leans. In the centre of this arrangement place a timepiece. Place it so, however, that anyone wishing to read the time, whether he wants to or not, must read my name.

'As far as the writing on this tomb goes – what do you think of this text: *Here rests C. Pompeius Trimalchio, a Maecenas. In spite of having held all offices, he desired none of them. He was devout, brave, faithful. His beginning was small, his end great. Thirty million talers he has left behind; and he never listened to a philosopher. Onlooker, farewell.*'

As he ended he spilled many tears. Fortunata wept and the whole roomful of guests first cried quietly and then howled. The noise filled the room as if they had already come to the wake. Thinking about my own death, even I had to cry awhile.

In all this sadness, Trimalchio wiped tears and salve out of his eyes, raised his arms, and cried with trembling mouth: 'Since we know so well that we all shall die, why not let us live! Come, you shall all be fortunate and happy. Come, let us throw ourselves into the bath.'

'Right, right,' said Habinnas. 'Let us make two days out of one.' He got up barefoot and followed Trimalchio, who was so drunk that he did not know which way his baths were.

We rose and walked out into a gallery. I turned to Ascyltos and asked him whether he knew where the baths were. I was in the middle of my question when a chained dog attacked him so viciously that he fell into a basin of goldfish. I, who was somewhat more sober, was trying to pull him out of reach of the dog's jaws, when I realised that the animal was painted into a fresco along the gallery. My conviction, however, changed again when I saw that Giton had wisely won the dog over to his side. Giton had thrown him all that he had eaten at the banquet, and thereby pacified him. Fortunately, before anything more could happen to us, the doorkeeper came and calmed the dog by his presence and chased him back into the fresco.

There was a ring at the door, and Mespoulets got up to see who it was. An old waiter with a tailcoat that a guest had ripped up the back had come to have it fixed.

Mespoulets told him that Lustgarten had left and sent him away. He turned a few pages and went on with *The Banquet*:

... Trimalchio pushed the youth away from himself, took his heavy silver drinking cup, and threw it at Fortunata, striking her full in the face with it. 'What does the wench think she is, that she can talk to me like that? I got her out of a bordello and brought her among decent people. Now she puffs herself up like a frog. I spit on her, on her bosom, on her abdomen. What does she think she is? A piece of wood she is – not a woman – but I suppose it is proper so. Out of a crow you can't make a dove. I will not go to bed until I have properly humbled this Cassandra.

'Listen to me,' he said, and tore her hands from her face. 'Listen you. When I was still a poor boy I could have wedded a woman who possessed a hundred thousand talers – do you hear? I suppose you know that this is no lie. Only yesterday, Agathon, who deals in salves and perfumes, took me aside and said to me: "I beg of you, don't let your name die. I have someone young and beautiful, who will serve you properly and bear you children – as many as you want." But, fool that I am, I am good and decent to you – I loved you – and here I strike myself with my own fist, that is how stupid I am,' he said.

'Ha, Fortunata, after my death, you will try to dig me out of the ground with your fingernails. You are going to see how stupidly you have behaved, you are going to be sorry, but it will be too late, forever too late. Habinnas, change the plans for my tomb. She shall not be on it. Remove her statue from it. She might want to argue with me after I am gone – and so that she shall know that I can punish, in the presence of all of you, I order here and now that when I am dead she shall not be allowed to kiss my corpse.'

Trimalchio suddenly began weeping like a child. 'Habinnas,' he said, 'if I have behaved badly, if I have said too much, go and spit in my face. I have kissed the best of my slaves a few times, not because he is so beautiful, but because he is so good of heart and because he is brave, faithful, honest, and devoted to me. He can recite ten discourses without losing a word, he can read his book without his tongue ever getting stuck, and the little gifts he receives he puts away into a small savings. He has saved up quite a respectable sum, this boy: I encourage his thrift – and isn't it proper that I have pleasure in seeing one so promising about me? But Fortunata can't bear it.'

Everyone was quiet, and he turned and said: 'But, my friends, let us have pleasure. Why be sad? Why worry! I beg you to enjoy yourselves. There was a time when I was but what you are today. Only through my intelligence have I come as far as I have. The brain, my friends, intelligence, makes men out of us – everything else is nonsense. I buy well and I sell well. Another may give you different advice, but that is the gist of it – and I am bursting with happiness.

'All that you see, all my happiness, is founded on thrift. When I came back from Asia I was no bigger than this golden candlestick here. I measured myself daily against it, and so that I should grow a beard soon, I rubbed oil out of the bowl of this lamp on my face every day. In the meantime I grew to be fourteen years old. I was the beloved, the pride of my master. Why shouldn't I tell you that? Why shouldn't I confess this? I think it is the first time I have told you. To obey the master, to do as he commands, nothing disgraceful in that, is there? But, besides, I also served the master's wife. I hope you understand me clearly. I made both of them happy. I will not go into it in detail – I am loathe to praise myself. The will of the gods removed them both and in the will of the master I was named sole heir. All this is a long story which I will spare you. Together with the emperor I shared his estate and took over his honours. But tell me, when ever has a man enough? I decided to buy ships.

'To make it brief, I equipped five ships and loaded them with wine, and that in those days was as good as currency, and sent them to Rome. As if I had ordered it all the five ships sank. On one day Neptune drank up three million talers. Do you think that I lost courage? No, by Hercules. I ordered larger, better, more fortunate ships to be built, so that everyone had to say, "There is a brave and fearless man." You know that the bigger the ships the stronger they are. When they were built I loaded them with bacon, with beans, with slaves, with wine, and with salve. In this part

of the story I must praise Fortunata's great loyalty. She sold
all her jewellery and her clothes and put the gold pieces
into my hand. What the gods desire happens quickly. On
one voyage I won a million. I got back my real estate, built
houses, bought cattle and teams. Whatever I touched grew
like stacks of honey cakes. At last, when I owned more than
my country did, I said, enough – and I changed. Away with
it, I said. I have enough of being a peddler. I got out of the
miserable business of buying and selling things and went
into banking. I advanced money to freemen and collected
interest. But just as I was about ready to drop my activities
altogether and retire – and my advice to you is never to
retire – a mathematician, a Greek, came into our colony.
He was a man of great intelligence. His name was Serapius.
He talked me into not giving it up. He sat down with me,
and in one long session he told me all about myself, things
that I had done and long ago forgotten. He recounted my
life for me from beginning to end; he knew all about me,
even about my intestines and the trouble I had with them.
He told me what I had eaten the day before. I could have
believed that from childhood on he had never been away
from my side.

'Weren't you there, Habinnas, when he said to me: "You
have found your wife in such-and-such a place. You are not
very fortunate in the choice of your friends. No one is going
to be grateful to you. You own wide stretches of land, but
you nourish a viper at your bosom." That is how he told

me everything – you remember, Habinnas. But to get back. Here we sit in this house. It was a hut when I bought it, and now I have made a palace out of it. As you all know, it contains four dining-rooms, twenty bedrooms, two marble galleries, and baths. In the upper storey are endless rooms for the servants, my own apartments, a boudoir for the viper there, a very good apartment for the doorkeeper, and a banquet hall for three hundred guests. The day Scaurus came here he would not put up anywhere except at my house – there is no other like it in the city.'

He stretched himself in his pillows and yawned. 'And that is how out of a frog a king was made.' He went on with the story, but it became so disgusting and repetitious that we looked at one another and then began to talk about other things. He was too drunk to know. All at once some musicians came and blew on their trumpets and, encouraged by Trimalchio, the band trumpeted so loud that the watchmen in that part of the town believed a fire had broken out. They came with axes and broke the doors open, carrying pails of water, and we took advantage of the opportunity, left him sleeping on his pillows, and ran away as fast as if the house of Agamemnon had really been on fire.

The story ended, Mespoulets went out into the library and put the book away on the classic side. The magician's dog turned three times on the blue coverlet at the foot of my bed; he curled up in comfort, his ears alert, his two clever eyes looking up.

Mespoulets sat and observed how often Trimalchio, in the reincarnation of a banker, a governor, a motor-car manufacturer, had told his story in this hotel.

He reminded me of the time when a guest had beaten up a woman, and called her all the names that Trimalchio had used. The slaves still carried out the large tables at the end of the banquet and brought in small ones. The waiters were still embraced by drunken hosts and promised their freedom: 'Here, Ambrose, you buy this stock tomorrow and I'll tell you when to sell it.'

In fact, there were only two details I could not find duplicated. One was the smart cook who made trees out of lard and the other was the magnificent tomb. Within six weeks after hearing the story I came across even these.

One day one of the cooks came up to the banquet office. Exactly like his counterpart nineteen hundred years before, he gave off the smells of fat and cooking and the scullery. He came because we wanted his advice. Some doctors were giving a party to two great surgeons who were brothers and ran a famous hospital, and they wanted to know whether it was possible, for a joke, to have some sweets passed after dinner in the shape of anatomical objects. The chef assured us that he had just the man for it. And a pastry cook, whose name was Didur, made what they wanted out of marzipan: fearful replicas of kidneys, hearts, eyes, tarsal bones, ears, and vertebrae. The grim *petits fours* were a great success. The cook was invited to come up and take a bow and was seated at the table. He was even photographed standing between the famous brother surgeons.

The tomb followed soon after. Instead of Trimalchio's arrangement with a clock, a banker made his memorial of nothing less than the stars. He presented a miraculous machine to the people – a black monster with two large bulbous heads on which eyes appear that project a parade of nine thousand stars, all the planets, the sun, and the moon. His name is mentioned now when people speak of the Planetarium and its marvellous machine – a machine so finely made that an operator can flick the constellations about at will, ahead for seven thousand years or back to the night of Trimalchio's banquet.

XV

The Murderer of the Splendide

Mespoulets fell apart both professionally and personally as the years went by. He was still in charge of the monkey-house, the dismal corner of the restaurant where the carpet was patched, where the service doors banged, where draughts of cold air came down from the ventilators directly overhead and cooking smells, mixed with the vapours of dish-water, came in warm waves from the kitchen. There, in the shadow of a dying palm tree, he functioned loudly and ineptly, breaking plates and glasses, spilling soup on people's sleeves, mixing up orders, and talking back to the guests. He was tired and miserable. In a dress suit shiny with the drippings of every soup and sauce on the menu, he could be seen leaning on a banister, biting his nails, looking into space, and waiting for the occasional undesirable customers whom Monsieur Victor sentenced to his tables. He made barely enough to live on and had moved from his furnished room in Chelsea to a cheaper one in Brooklyn. It was hard to find anyone to work with him; no bus boy wanted to share the meagre tips or suffer the abuse of Mespoulets. Once kind and patient, he had become like a mean old dog. I was afraid that Mespoulets would be fired any day.

The firing of employees usually took place about nine in the morning. At that time every day, Monsieur Victor arrived in a short, black coat and striped trousers, sat down at a table in the empty dining-room, drank a cup of English breakfast tea, ate a brioche, and smoked a few Dimitrinos. His secretary brought him the mail and sat at a table nearby, ready to take down whatever orders he might have to give. His first assistant hovered around respectfully. The manager of the banquet department and myself were responsible directly to Monsieur Victor, and it was our duty to hover around also at this hour. Captains, waiters, and bus boys who were in trouble were called in and made to stand before Monsieur Victor, and a kind of court-martial was held. Victor, an expert at inflicting pain, moved his chair back and announced his findings slowly and usually with a smile. He treated the culprits to short, exquisite essays on promptness, on the relations between guest and waiter, on service, and on the particular circumstances of their cases. He loved to do this with deliberation. His essays nearly always ended in discharge. His judgments were absolute and final. He wished no advice, no defence of his victims, no recommendations for clemency, and, above all, no explanations.

It was no surprise to me when one morning while Monsieur Victor was opening his mail, he smiled, looked up at me, and then, as he started to read a letter, said, 'Go call Mespoulets. I am going to fire your friend. He is—' But there he stopped. He put the letter he had just opened into his pocket and abruptly dismissed all those present. I started to leave the restaurant and he got up from his table, ran after me, took my arm, and said, 'Come here. Have a look at this.' Behind a screen near the sickly palm under which Mespoulets's tables stood, he showed me the letter he had put in his pocket. It was a sheet of yellow paper decorated with daggers and skulls and a bleeding heart. Under this was printed in crude letters, 'YOU ARE DOOMED, MONSIEUR VICTOR.' Monsieur Victor looked doomed; he no longer smiled; his voice had changed. He read the words over and over, looked at the drawings, held the paper against the light, and then looked at the envelope. It was postmarked 'Brooklyn'. 'What do you think of it?' he asked me. 'Should I call the police? My God, I have never – what do you think?' I said that I thought it was a joke. At that moment Mespoulets came in with an armful of table-cloths and began to put them on his tables, smoothing them out with his hands. He made a deep bow and said, '*Bonjour*, M'sieur Victor.' Monsieur Victor, who hardly ever spoke directly to an employee except to reprimand him and answered all greetings with a curt nod of his head, said, '*Bonjour*, Mespoulets.' I thought he might be in the proper mood for leniency, and I asked him if, as a favour to me, he would let me take Mespoulets over into the banquet department, where I could give him a simple job in which his shortcomings would not be noticeable.

'Of course, of course,' he said. 'But about this – about the letter – should I call the police? Don't you think it would be better if I did? No, no,' he answered himself. 'I think you are right. It's a joke.' He tore the letter up. Then he put the pieces together and read the message once more, shoved it into his pocket, and went to his office. Two more letters with the same decorations, the same warning of doom for Monsieur Victor, and the same Brooklyn postmark arrived that week, and Monsieur Victor remained nervous and subdued. No one was fired for days, and Mespoulets became a waiter in the banquet department.

The waiters who are engaged to work at banquets need not be as swift, as intelligent, or as presentable as those who serve in the restaurants of a hotel such as the Splendide. Their duties are much simpler. At a banquet, each waiter has one table. At that table are seated eight guests, who naturally all eat the same things at the same time. A signal – usually a green light somewhere near the ceiling – is given by the banquet head waiter when the guests are to be served a new course, and the signal also tells the waiters when the plates are to be changed for the next course. Banquet menus are, with rare exceptions, unimaginative and repetitious. The waiters are a kind of conveyer belt that runs from kitchen to guests and then out into the pantry, loaded with the dirty dishes. They line up in front of the various counters, in turn, outside in the banquet kitchen; at one counter they get the fruit cocktail, at another the soup, then the fish, then the roast, the vegetables, the salad, and finally the dessert, the *petits fours*, and the coffee. Captains stand everywhere to keep them in line and tell them where to go. It is all cut and dried. The people on the dais, at the speakers' table, or, in the case of weddings, the immediate family, are served by a few well-trained men. The rest are extras hired for the night. Although Mespoulets was worse than most of the extras, I put him on the regular payroll and assigned him to a table in the ballroom, where the big banquets were held. His table was just a few steps away from the pantry. He was teamed up with a younger waiter, another Frenchman, named Ladame, and it seemed to be working out about as well as I had expected.

Every large hotel has among its waiters a group of malcontents. They congregate in groups in the pantries while they wait to serve; they stand in the kitchen or pantry and discuss the state of the world. In those days the Germans argued about their German problems; the Italians, in another group, waved their napkins in the air and shouted and made wild-eyed predictions. Mespoulets was soon the leader of the discontented Frenchmen. He was articulate, he had Communistic ideas, and in his harangues he rescued a few ominous *bons mots* from his failing memory. '*Écrasez l'infâme!*' he would shout. The nervous French waiters who were in his group sometimes thought him too violent. The Germans and Italians would come up and listen to him. The pantry rang with his eloquence, and often I had to send a captain to tell him to be quiet, because the noise could be heard inside the ballroom above the voices of the speakers. Even the waiters sometimes said, 'Sh-h-h! Quiet, Mespoulets.'

When the signal to serve was given, Mespoulets usually came down from his pulpit, the second step of the pantry stairway, and ran to get a tray of dishes. Trembling, mumbling, and excited, he walked into the ballroom and served his guests. Then he retired to a corner, wiped the sweat from his forehead with a napkin instead of his handkerchief, and bit his nails until the little green light gave the signal to clear off. He would not see it, but his partner, Ladame, would say, 'All right, Mespoulets, clear off,' and Mespoulets would clear off.

Mespoulets was moody. For several days at a time he would seem to be happy, almost elated. Around his mouth played a smile of self-satisfaction, and he talked confidently to the other waiters. From this mood he would sink into a torpid, sullen state and complain of severe headaches. One time, after a long speech to the other waiters, he fell on the floor of the pantry in a faint. He lay with his eyes wide open and his hands turned into claws. When he came to, I got the house physician to look at him. The doctor said he just needed a few days' rest. I sent him to his room in Brooklyn in a taxicab and told him to stay there until he felt well again.

About a week later, he came back. After what had happened, I could no longer employ him as a waiter, but he could be used on other, easier jobs. I made him a captain. I thought there could be no waiter so dumb or so old that he could fail as a captain in the banquet department. A captain in the banquet department has a black tie instead of a white one, and for the rest, he nods to guests as they come in and smiles and shows people where the ladies' and gentlemen's rooms are – 'Downstairs to the left, Madame. Downstairs to the right, Monsieur.' He is engaged chiefly for decorative purposes, and the only other thing he has to do is pass the cigars while the coffee is being served. Mespoulets, however, proved he could not be trusted even with these duties. He did not take any cigars for himself, but he became absent-minded and passed them to the ladies. He gave both ladies and gentlemen the wrong directions. He also had more time for his speeches now, and kept the waiters out in the pantry instead of at their stations. So this appointment, too, was proved a mistake. I had to take his black tie away from him and give him a job in which he did not come in contact with the guests.

He was assigned to order rolls and butter when they were needed and to see that the musicians got their water, coffee, and sandwiches. The rest of the time he was an unofficial watchman at doors through which people could crash a party.

On one such watchman's assignment he stood up on a balcony overlooking the ballroom. On this balcony was a door which could not be locked, since it served as an emergency exit in case of fire. This was a favourite door for crashers, and also for dishwashers and other employees who were curious, who wanted to listen to music or occasionally to the speeches. It was the watchman's duty to see that no one came in through that door.

A dinner was given one evening for a distinguished French author, an Academician whose writings were of a political character. The ballroom was filled with very important guests; some of them had come from Washington. At the speakers' table presided Dr Finley of the *Times*. In the audience were Otto Kahn, Barney Baruch, Secretary Lansing. French and American flags were on the tables, an orchestra was engaged to play during the reception, ending with the anthems of both countries. Dinner was at eight sharp, speeches after the coffee, everything over by midnight.

Just before the speeches began, I walked up to the balcony to see if Mespoulets was watching his door. He was leaning against it and biting his nails, and when he saw me, he pointed below and said, 'Give me two machine guns, one on this side and the other over on the other side. I'll cover the doors and get them as they try to get out, just like with a hose up and down – *brrrrrr* – and the other gun can spray the speakers' table – *brrrrr* – *brrrrr* – *brrrrrr*, Table No. 1 – *brrrrr*, Table No. 2 – aim for the plates, shoot through the table, hit them in the stomach so they suffer awhile. Here are our enemies. *Écrasez l'infâme,*' he almost shouted. '*Liberté, égalité, fraternité!* Ah! What has become of you? What mockery! Look there! They're all crooks!'

'All right, Mespoulets, go home,' I said, and put another watchman in his place.

Since Mespoulets was a good penman, I gave him a job we had open for a man to make out lists of material that had to be ordered for banquets – long sheets of paper on which were printed the many things one needs to serve a mass of people. The lists started with demitasse spoons and ended with how many buckets of fine ice and cube ice had to be ordered to cool champagne, to shake up in cocktails, at what time all this had to be delivered, and to what pantry. Besides this, checks had to be sent out for various supplies which the department bought. To this job we assigned Mespoulets, and he did his work to everyone's satisfaction. He seemed very happy to have escaped into a job in which, he said, he was a gentleman and could use his mind. He kept clerical hours now, washed his hands at five, and at five-thirty went home. There was peace for a while in the ballroom. Below, in the restaurant, the letters on yellow paper decorated with daggers, guns, and bleeding hearts, and more recently with bombs blowing up tables and chairs, kept arriving regularly.

Monsieur Victor had begun to get used to them, but he was still a little nervous. Von Kyling, the banquet manager, had shown them to the police captain of our precinct, who said that they were clearly from a dangerous man. The police captain asked if any of us had any suspicions as to who the writer of the letters might be, and von Kyling said that it could be any one of a thousand or so employees whom Monsieur Victor had fired, or even one of the innumerable undesirable guests of the hotel whom he had insulted in the course of many years. The police captain said in that case he could be of little help. Monsieur Victor continued to examine the letters and show them to us when they came in, but none of us could think of anything to do about them. His secretary kept on filing them away.

Late one afternoon, Ladame, the French waiter who had been teamed with Mespoulets in the ballroom, came to me with the face of one who is burdened. He twisted and squeezed a napkin in his hands and moved a chair and finally asked for a few words with me alone. He asked for my strict confidence, and then, looking around several times and leading me to a dim corner of the ballroom, told me that he did not wish to turn informer but he felt he had to tell me, and that he told me because I was a friend of Mespoulets and had always helped him, and so on, and that he told me only because he was worried. He finally whispered that Mespoulets had said if he, Ladame, would bring him his telephone and gas and electric-light bills, he would see to it that they were paid. Mespoulets had explained that he was the secretary of the banquet department now, and sent out checks, and that he would arrange to mix these bills with invoices and have them O.K.'d and paid. It was perfectly all right to do this, Mespoulets had said, because the hotel oppressed and exploited its employees. Monsieur Victor, who was rich, was particularly tyrannical and this was just one little way in which he could make things even. To how many men Mespoulets had offered this assistance, Ladame did not know.

When I went to look for Mespoulets, I found he had gone home. I asked the night auditor to come over and we went through the invoices. We found several irregularities – checks Mespoulets had sent out for small sums, like two dollars and thirty-five cents, a dollar eighty, and the highest for four dollars and thirty-six cents. I asked the auditor to keep the matter quiet for the time being.

Early the next day I looked for Mespoulets again. I could tell that he had come to work because his hat and coat were in the employees' cloakroom, but he was not at his desk.

I walked all over the hotel in search of him. He was not in any of the large rooms, or down among the waiters' dressing rooms, where he sometimes hung out. He was not in the employees' barber shop or at one of the tables in the staff dining room, where he now took his meals. I looked for him in the private dining-rooms, the pantries, and in the Jade Suite. He was not there either.

The architectural waste that goes with the building of the elaborate public apartments of a luxury hotel creates many odd corners. A semicircular dining-room, a flight of stairs from one elevation to another, rotundas and balconies – in, under, and around all these are vacant spaces which are used as lockers for brooms, vacuum-cleaning equipment, extra tables, and spare pieces of furniture. We had dozens of these closets. Mespoulets was in none of them.

At the south side of the ballroom, under the stage, was a long corridor. The electricians went in there sometimes to replace fuses or to connect cables for projection machines when movies were to be shown. The parts of a long horseshoe table were stored in there as well. On one side of this passage were switches and boxes with fuses, and on the other was a row of steel doors, behind which the elevators passed up and down, sucking in air and rattling the doors. The place was filled with the breathing of the heavy machinery, a mechanical intake and outgo, and a machine somewhere far below pounded in even rhythm like a beating heart. I walked in there and saw Mespoulets at the other end. He was leaning against a steel door, holding his head with both hands and howling like an animal. He had not heard me come in and he did not see me go.

It all fitted together now – the speeches, the feeling of persecution exhibited in the petty embezzlements, the resentment of Monsieur Victor, the fainting spell, the periods of elation and depression, and now this hysteria. I remembered all the way back to when I was his bus boy and how I went home with him one day and saw him cut his canary's head off. Mespoulets lived in Brooklyn, and he was obviously the man who had been writing the letters.

I went to Monsieur Victor's secretary and asked her to give me the letters. A new one had arrived a few days before. On the yellow paper there was again the bleeding heart, the dagger filled in with red ink to the hilt, and a scene in which a bomb blew up tables and chairs. The chairs in the restaurant of the Splendide were of peculiar construction, very costly, and styled unlike the chairs in any other restaurant. Even in the crude fashion in which the chairs on the yellow paper were drawn, they clearly resembled our chairs. Someone who knew these chairs well and had worked among them was writing and illustrating the letters. Every protecting doubt vanished. The last letter was signed in something of a brownish shade. It was more violent and confused than any of the others had been.

Without telling either Monsieur Victor or von Kyling, I took the packet of letters and went to see the head of the psychiatric department of one of the city's largest hospitals, a man who often came to the hotel and with whom I was acquainted. He looked at them carefully and began to read them. Soon he became interested and started to nod his head. He thought that the last one was probably signed with blood. He swung his chair around and said, 'This man is a killer.' I asked him if anything could be done about the situation, and he said, 'Sometimes – if there is a close relative willing to sign a commitment to an insane asylum. Has this man any relatives?'

'He has, as far as I know, a daughter who lives in France – Marseille,' I said.

'There you are,' he said. 'Without a relative, you can do very little. If you had a business out and away from everywhere, then, between you and me, I'd advise you to run him over with a truck and make it look like an accident. As it is, there's nothing much you can do. The laws governing the legal commitment of such people are themselves psychopathic. Why, only last year, twenty-one such cases were brought to me right here in this hospital. I had to release every one of them, identical cases, exactly like this one. Up to this moment seven of them have done murder, and I am waiting for the others. Under the law, you need a relative to commit them. It's practically impossible to have them put away without a relative. The law is on the side of these maniacs. If they go before a lunacy commission, they usually blossom out and talk like philosophers. This man is safe as long as he can take it out in writing letters, but God help you if he runs out of red ink. Whatever you do, don't annoy him, and for heaven's sake don't fire him.

'There's always this comfort. Last year one of these fellows chased me all over the lobby of a hotel in Milwaukee. He fired four times and missed me three. The fourth shot was only a flesh wound.' The doctor pulled up his right trouser leg and showed me a scar just below his knee. 'They get into a high state of excitement, and the motor reactions are interfered with, and for that reason he may quite possibly miss you.'

The psychiatrist gave me back the letters, and at the elevator he said once more, 'And don't forget, whatever you do, don't fire him, and try not to provoke him.'

I went back to the hotel as quickly as I could and ran up to the ballroom. As I passed through the outer office, I saw that Mespoulets's desk was still vacant. But instead of the usual disorder, the ink, pens, and blotters were neatly arranged, and the books and various forms he used for ordering material had been put away. I asked von Kyling where Mespoulets was, and he said that Monsieur Victor had found out about the checks and had fired him just before lunch.

'How did he take it?' I asked.

'He didn't say a word – just nodded, and went and got his hat and coat and left,' said von Kyling.

I went over to the restaurant and asked Monsieur Victor to come to the ballroom, where we could talk privately. I gave him back the letters and told him what the doctor at the hospital had said. Monsieur Victor sat down. His face twitched and he said, 'Oh God, oh God, oh my *God*!' He wanted to call the police, but, afraid of the bad publicity this might bring to the Splendide, he instead gave orders to the timekeeper not to let Mespoulets into the hotel. He stationed a *maître d'hôtel* at the entrance to the lobby and another in the pantry, and before he went to his office he called up his secretary and asked, 'Is everything all right over there?' 'Yes, everything is all right over here,' she answered. He looked around corners as he left the office, slowly walked out into the open ballroom, ran down to the restaurant, and, in spite of all these precautions, complained of a headache and went home right after lunch.

He came to see von Kyling and me the next morning in the ballroom office before he had his brioche and coffee. He said that he had not been able to close an eye all night.

Von Kyling told him that he had privately consulted the police captain again, and he had said that they might pick up Mespoulets and hold him for a while for leading a Communist demonstration, but that eventually they would have to let him go. The man, he said, had his constitutional rights. Of course, after he had shot somebody, they would move right in on him. 'But that,' said Monsieur Victor, 'would be small consolation to my family.'

He had a drink, then called up his office, and asked, as he had the day before, 'Is everything all right over there?' and his secretary answered that everything was all right. He took one more drink and went over to his office.

Von Kyling and I sat down. Von Kyling was a quiet man and always did the thinking when we were in any difficulty. He was bald on top of his head and over each ear was a patch of grey hair which he let grow very long. When he thought hard he twisted these hairs into curls. He had not slept either.

'Before we do anything,' said von Kyling, 'we want to find out how Mespoulets feels about this. We'll get hold of Ladame and send him over to Mespoulets's house. Ladame is to tell him that he is very indignant at his discharge and he is to try and find out how Mespoulets feels about it.'

We sent Ladame over to Brooklyn. He came back and said that he had found Mespoulets sitting at a table, talking to himself and drinking brandy. He had bitten his fingernails, refused to answer questions, and looked out of the window.

When Ladame had left, von Kyling said to me, 'Listen carefully, and tell me how this sounds to you. The telephone bills and the gas and electric-light bills were paid with company checks. You go over with Ladame and see Mespoulets. He trusts you. You tell him that you have come to warn him. Say that the company has put the whole thing into the hands of the police and that the police are on the way to his house, but because you are his friend, you have come to warn him and help him to get away. We have to get him on a boat, get him out of the country. Once he's out, he can't come back. He's not even got his first papers.'

For the next hour, von Kyling was busy telephoning. With the aid of the hotel's steamship agent, he found the office of a travel bureau which specialised in trips on tramp steamers. Their downtown office informed us of four boats that were leaving at dawn the next day. The most suitable of these seemed to be the twelve-thousand-ton cargo boat *Sadi Carnot*, sailing from Brooklyn for Marseille. There was no time to lose. While von Kyling arranged for the passage, Ladame and I went to see Mespoulets in his rooming-house. We found him bent over a table in his room. He listened quietly. We did not mention the letters and neither did he. He thanked us for our efforts to save him from the police, we helped him pack, and then we sent a cable to his daughter Mélanie to meet the boat in Marseille. We took him out to a late dinner, gave him more to drink, and put him on his ship towards morning. In his stateroom, we helped him into bed, left him some money, and sat with him as he fell asleep. We left him just before the boat sailed at sunrise.

As soon as Monsieur Victor walked into the hotel that morning, he called von Kyling up and asked whether everything was all right, then asked us to come over to his office. He listened quietly to our report of what we had done with Mespoulets. When he had been troubled, he had become cordial. Now he was himself again. He spoke in the pompous, somewhat mincing tones that he affected with his guests; he divided his attention between the telephone and a list of reservations beside which he was writing table numbers. He had realised that we might ask him for a contribution towards the cost of disposing of Mespoulets, so now, without asking what this sum was, he suggested that it might be broken up and charged against sundry operating expenses. He hummed softly to himself and disappeared among his tables, placing reservation cards here and there.

Monsieur Victor's reprieve from anxiety was brief. A week later, at the customary morning court-martial for employees about to be fired, Victor was opening his mail and prolonging the sentencing of a bus boy with a little essay on service when he flung down a half-opened envelope. Protruding from an envelope was the familiar yellow paper, and when we unfolded the letter, there was the bleeding heart once more and the warning, 'YOU ARE DOOMED, MONSIEUR VICTOR.' The letter had been mailed the night before, in Brooklyn.

To the One I Love the Best

Ludwig Bemelmans

———— • ————

Ludwig Bemelmans came to the California home of famed interior decorator Elsie de Wolfe, Lady Mendl, for cocktails. By the end of the night, he was firmly established as a member of the family: given a bedroom in their sumptuous house, and invitations to the most outrageous parties in Hollywood.

With hilarity and mischief, Bemelmans lifts the curtain on a bygone world of extravagance, where the parties are held in circus tents and populated by ravishing movie stars. *To the One I Love the Best* is a luminous painting of life's oddities and a touching tribute to a fabulously eccentric woman.